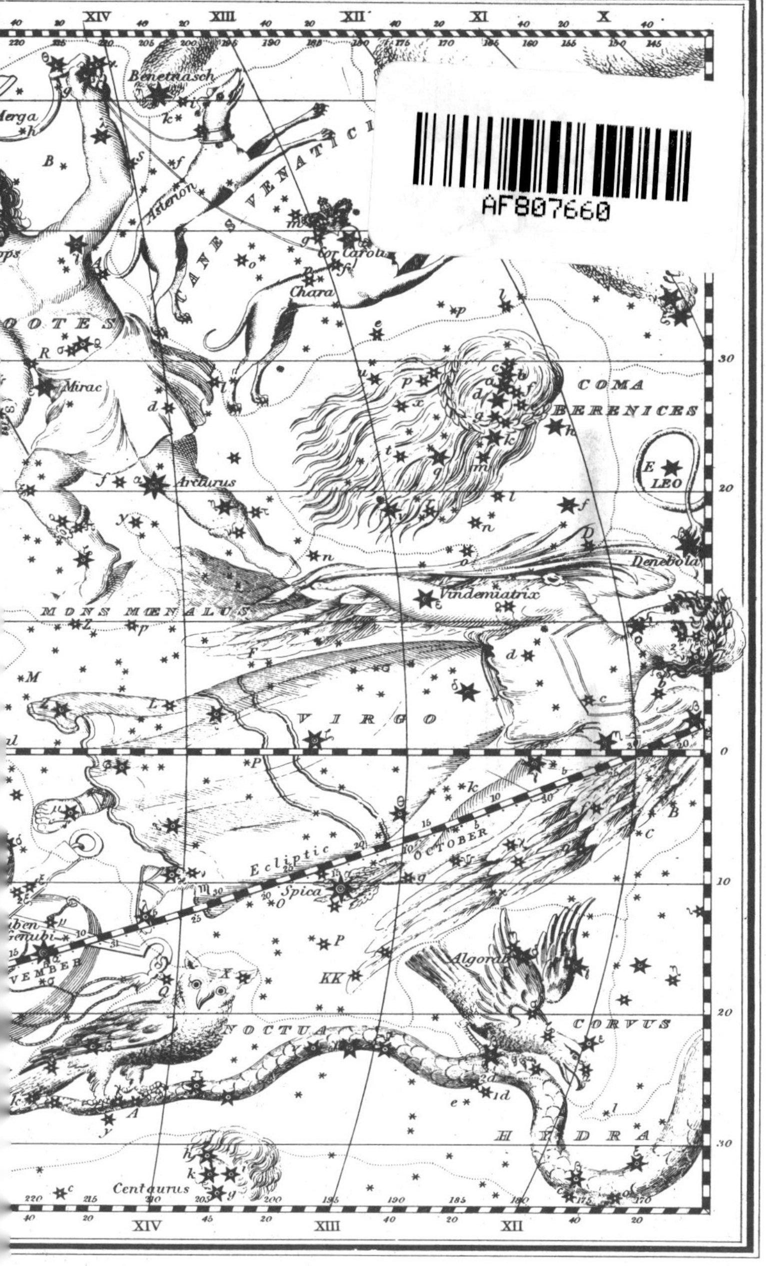
XIV
XIII
XII
XI
X
Benetnasch
Merga
Asterion
CANES VENATICI
Cor Caroli
Chara
BOOTES
Mirac
Arcturus
COMA
BERENICES
LEO
Denebola
Vindemiatrix
MONS MŒNALUS
VIRGO
Ecliptic
OCTOBER
Spica
Algorab
CORVUS
NOCTUA
HYDRA
Centaurus
NOVEMBER

A flock of sheep that leisurely pass by
One after one; the sound of rain and bees
Murmuring, the fall of rivers, wind and seas,
Smooth Fields, white sheets of water, and pure sky:
I've thought of all by turns, and still I lie
Sleepless; and soon the small birds' melodies
Must bear, first uttered from my orchard trees,
And the first cuckoo's melancholy cry.
Even thus last night, and two nights more, I lay,
And could not win thee, Sleep, by any stealth,
So do not let me wear to-night away;
Without thee what is all the morning's wealth?
Come, blessed barrier between day and day,
Dear Mother of fresh thoughts and joyous health.

—William Wordsworth (1770-1850)

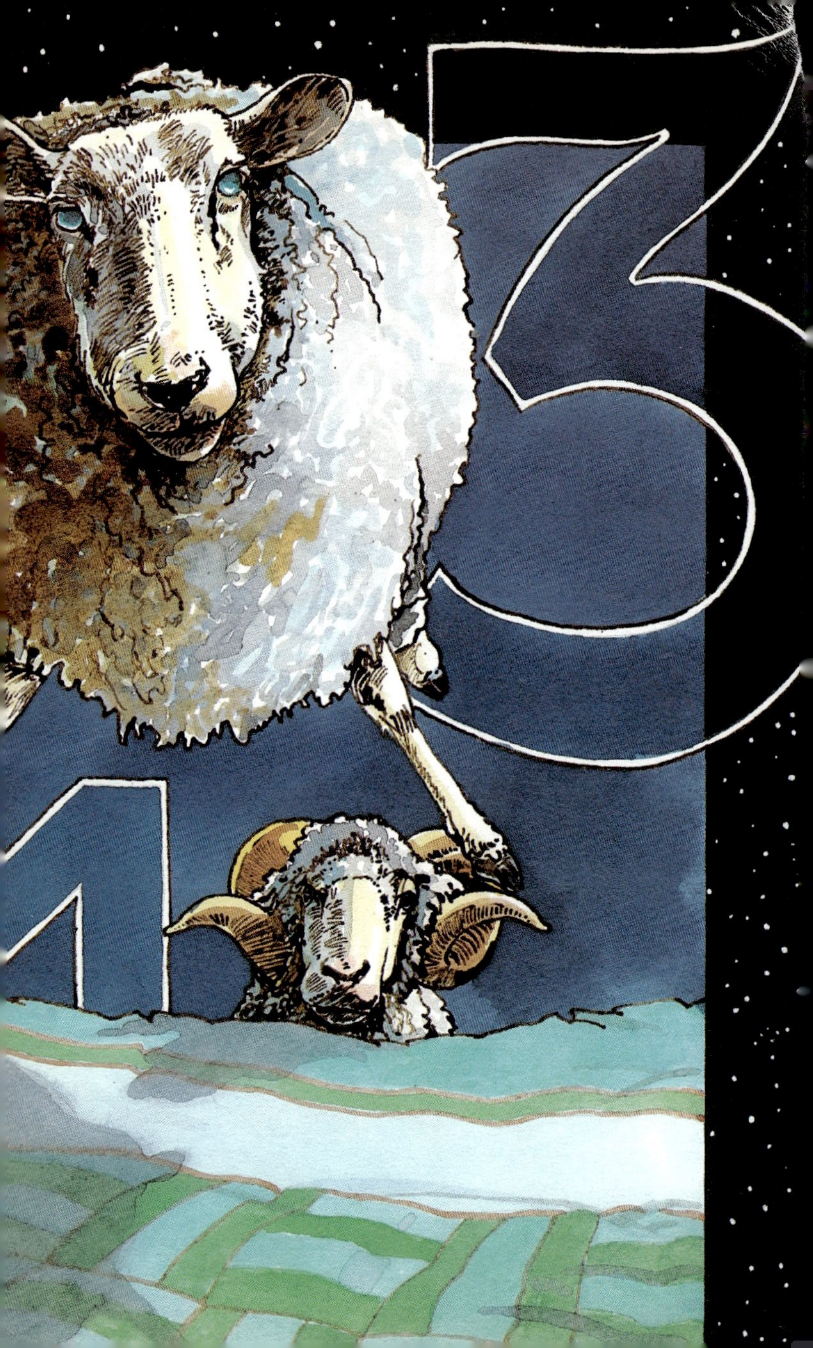

GRAPHIS

COUNTING SHEEP

A BOOK TO FALL ASLEEP WITH

EDITED BY: B. MARTIN PEDERSEN
EDITORS: ANNETTE CRANDALL, HEINKE JENSSEN, JACK CRAGER
ART DIRECTORS: B. MARTIN PEDERSEN, RANDELL PEARSON
CONSTELLATION ILLUSTRATION: JENNIFER THORPE

To parody a line from "To His Coy Mistress" by Andrew Marvell (1621–78): "The bed's a fine and private place/If sleep and I do there embrace/But when we don't its like a grave/In which I toss and turn depraved." This book is a paean to two of the traditional calming stratagems and visual incantations which we desperate humans have devised over the ages to win release into the arms of Morpheus from such a grave. And so you, dear bedtime reader (or otherwise), please turn the pages to enumerate the stars and their constellations and, in particular, count the sheep, the many many sheep—jumping or not over every possible kind of STILE, be it baroque, rococo, empire, impressionist, art nouveau or deco. ❍ But why sheep? Perhaps the rhyming resemblance of that word to "sleep" confers on it a special somnolent suggestiveness. Perhaps it is the innumerableness of sheep in flocks that lends to the mantra-like act of counting them the mindless repetitiousness necessary to block from consciousness the worries, tensions, and pesky self-awarenesses so antithetical to sleep. Thomas Beers, in speaking of "the soft enrobing of the fleecy folds of sleep," may have captured in that delicious metaphor the suggestive appeal of evoking sheep in the pursuit of sleep. ❍ When did the practice of counting sheep begin? Probably back in the mists of time when sheep were a common symbol in a primarily agrarian culture, but certainly by Wordsworth's era. However, the tallying not of just sheep but of jumping sheep was apparently first mentioned in print only in 1854. Seba Smith in his short story, "The Dutch Wedding" from WAY DOWN EAST published that year, says of the bridegroom on the eve of his marriage: "He shut his eyes with all his might and tried to think of sheep jumping over a wall; but do all he could, sleep wouldn't come." ❍ What's the problem with sleep's not coming? According to a Gallup Poll conducted for the National Sleep Foundation, insomnia is credited with producing or exacerbating concentration difficulties, irritability, and other emotional problems affecting one's love life or on-the-job interactions. Also, a higher rate of automobile accidents are caused by the decreased vigilance associated with insomnia than by drunken driving. That's a lot of problem, given that approximately one-third of our population suffers from insomnia, a quarter of that third having it severely and chronically. ❍ What are the causes of insomnia? Obviously, tensions and worries are major culprits, including the worry over not being able to sleep, itself. A few people suffer from "pseudoinsomnia" in which they think that they are lying in bed trying to fall asleep but are in reality only dreaming it. Another cause of insomnia, occasionally of real medical concern, is SLEEP APNEA. This inability to sleep and breathe at the same time results in brief awakenings during the night to catch one's breath but of which no memory is retained. It is often evidenced by bouts of loud snoring and an inexplicable fatigue on awakening in the morning. But the chief cause of insomnia these days is sleeping medication itself. Unless responsibly prescribed and monitored, sleeping medication can lead to a drug-dependency insomnia and a vicious cycle of taking even more sleeping medication. For the most part, counting sheep or stars is more effective or certainly safer. Better yet are the relaxation therapies and other treatments now available from licensed sleep clinics and therapists. ○ The craving for sleep, if unfulfilled, is only exceeded in its unpleasantness by intense pain. In the Korean War, an effective brainwashing technique used to persuade captured American servicemen to change their political beliefs was the withholding of sleep until they did. Given enough motivation, however, remarkable feats of voluntary resistance to sleep are possible. One 17-year-old boy stayed awake for 264 hours in order to earn a place in the GUINNESS BOOK OF WORLD RECORDS. Afterwards, he slept for a little less than 15 hours and awoke feeling fine. ○ Then why is sleep demanded of us all on a regular basis? One hypothesis is that sleep evolved in vertebrates as an invention of Nature for keeping us out of harm's way at those times of the day-night cycle when being awake is relatively useless in terms of finding food or a mate and thus needlessly exposes us to our predators. Perhaps this explains why a clocking mechanism exists in our brains which, even in the absence of light-dark cues, wakes us at times coinciding with growing daylight and makes us bed down as night approaches. This mechanism tends to operate on a 25-hour cycle, which is reset from day to day by light-dark cues; in our light-bulb dominated modern society it is flexible enough to accommodate both night-owls and early risers. Resetting this mechanism to a drastically new schedule, though, can take several days, as those who have suffered jet-lag well know. ○ Another reason we sleep for a third of our lives is that we need to spend a certain amount of time each night dreaming. Judging from the rapid eye movements (REMs) that symptomize a narrative dream, it is now known that we dream in several bouts during the night, separated from each other by roughly 90 minutes. These bouts get longer toward morning and the eye movements are highly correlated with the action being observed in the dreams. Quite puzzling, however, is the fact that, according to their REMs, even newborn infants dream and do so almost incessantly, but of what—cherub land from whence they came? Research suggests that dreaming is but the tip of an iceberg of extreme brain arousal exceeding that of the waking day. In that phase of sleep, the brain consolidates what it has experienced and learned during the preceding period of wakefulness with what it already knows. ○ "So get on with your sheep/Then get on with your sleep/In the quite secure comfort of what lies in store/Sweet dreams—not insomniac wolves at your door." ○

–EDGAR E. COONS, PHD.

PROFESSOR OF PSYCHOLOGY AND NEUROSCIENCE, NEW YORK UNIVERSITY

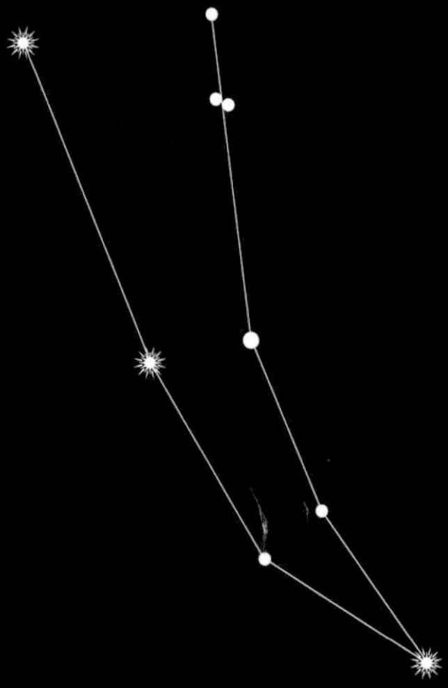

Andromeda

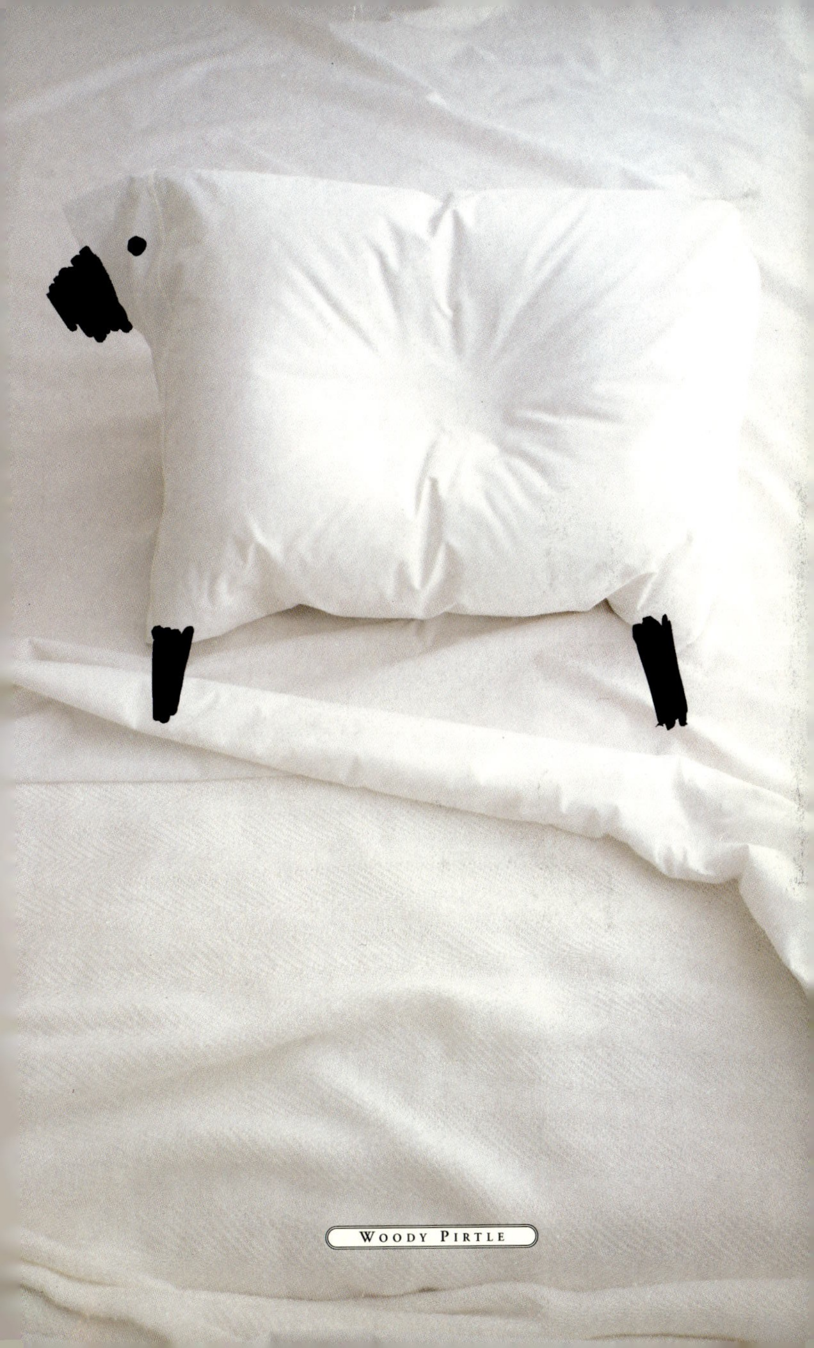
Woody Pirtle

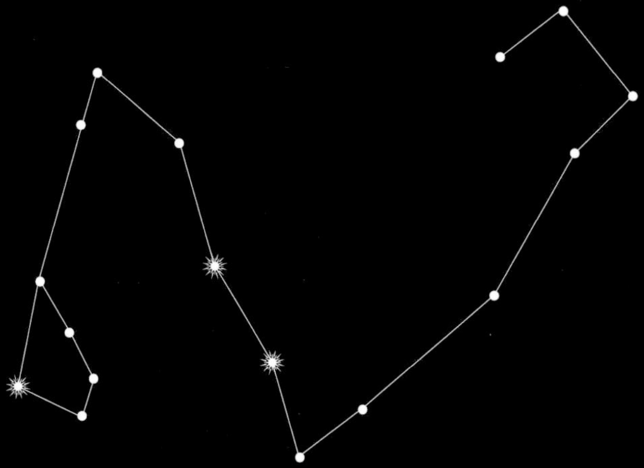

Hydra the Sea Serpent

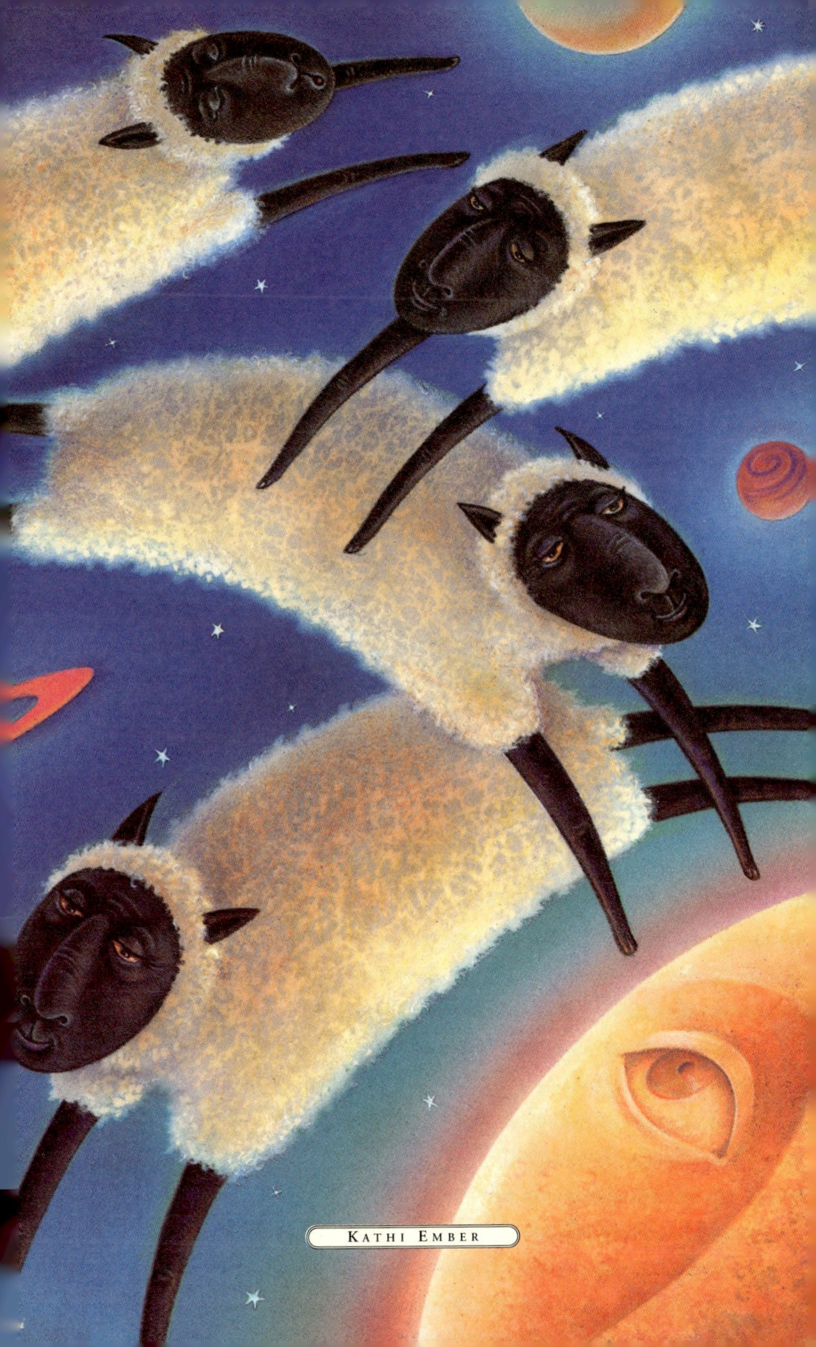
KATHI EMBER

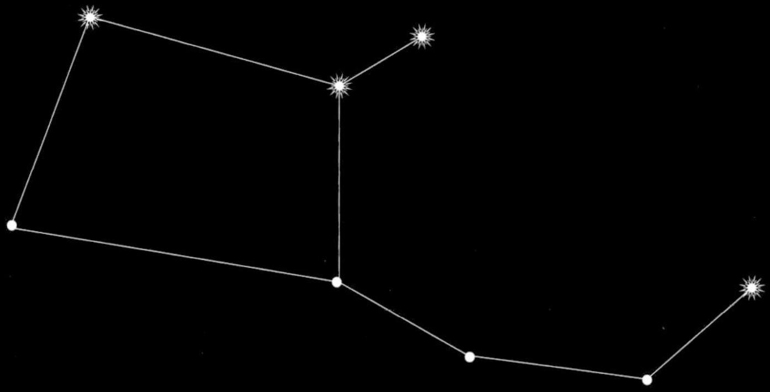

Pegasus

11

ELEVEN

ELF

ONZE

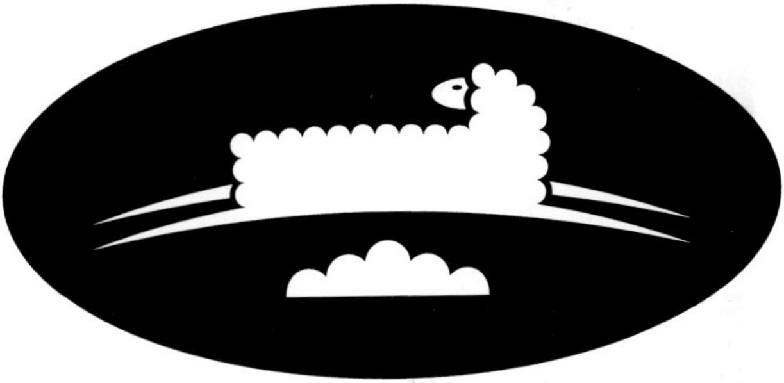

DIANA MCKNIGHT

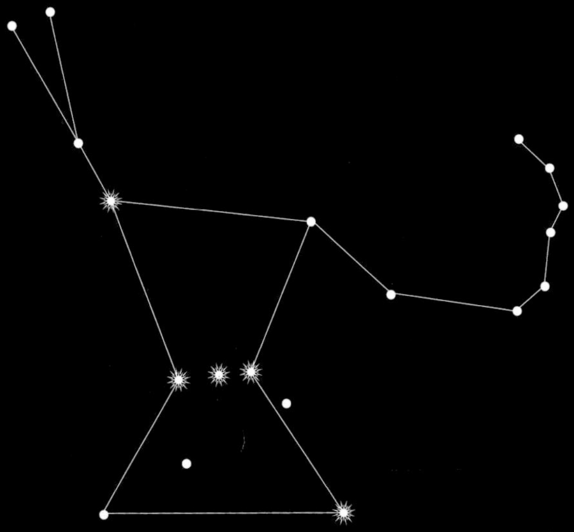

Orion the Hunter

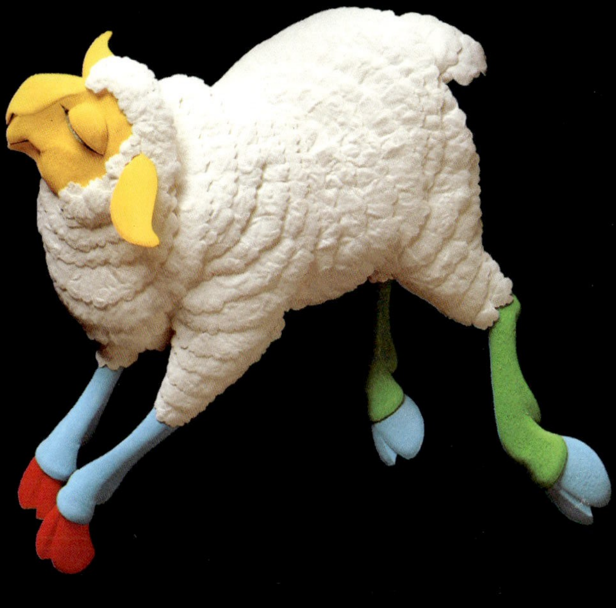

JONATHAN MILNE

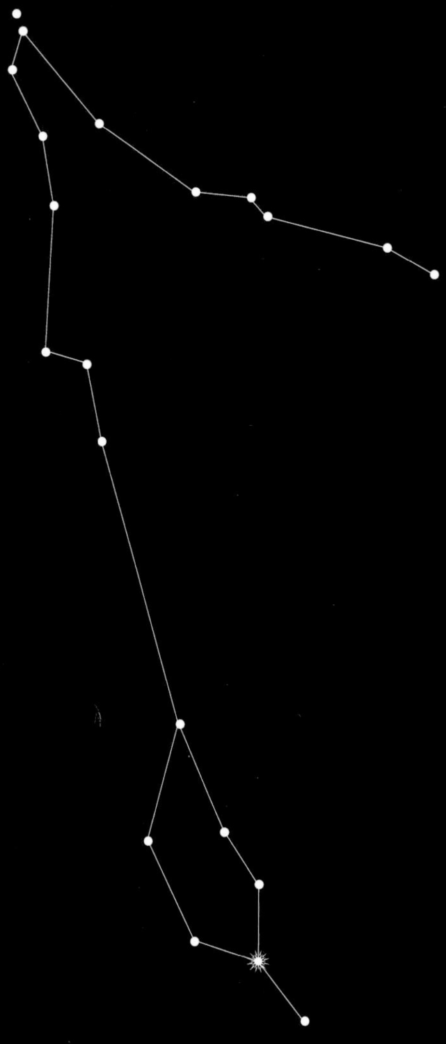

Pisces the Fish

SHEEP

SHEEP

SLEEP

Craig Cook

Z Z Z Z

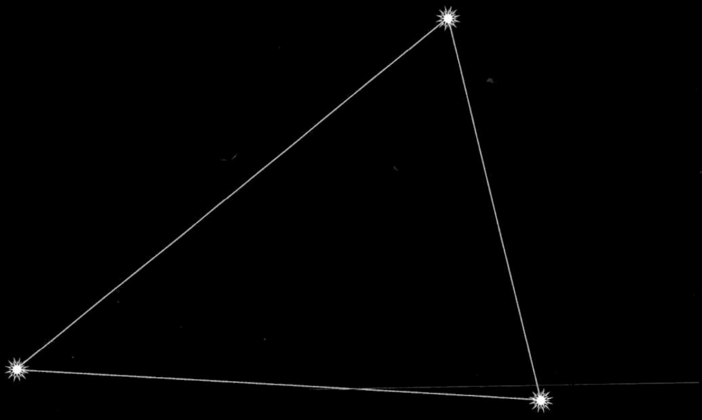

Summer Triangle

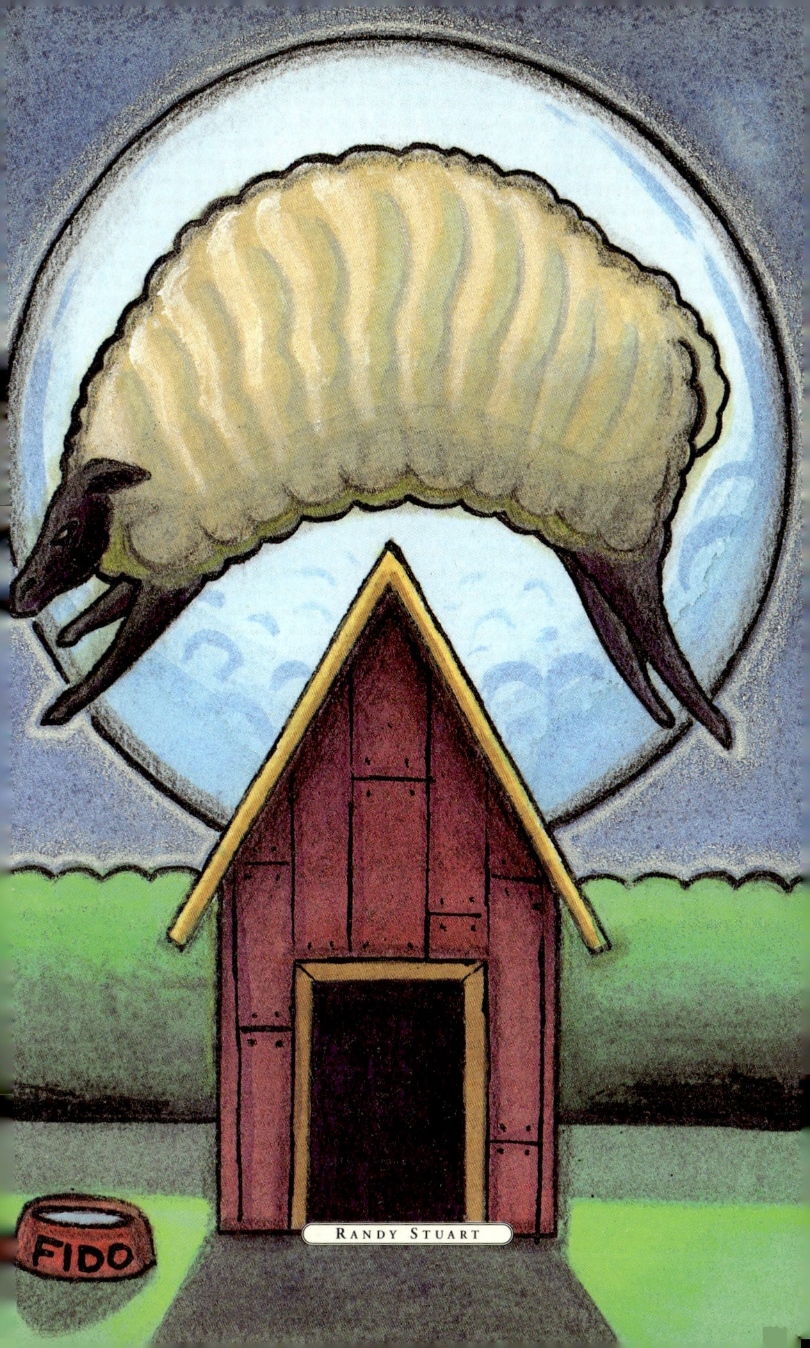
FIDO
RANDY STUART

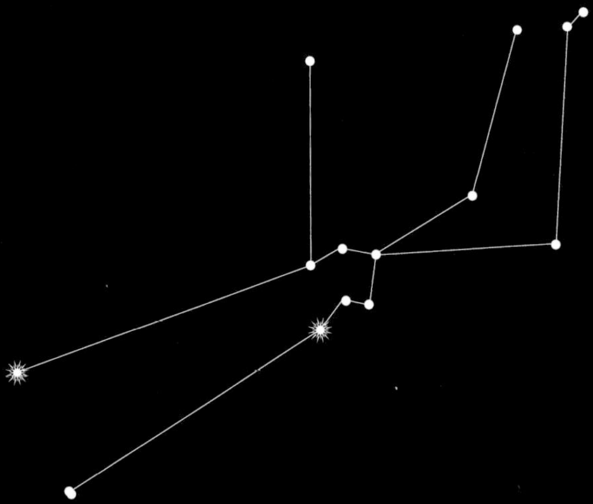

Taurus the Bull

19

NINETEEN

NEUNZEHN

DIX-NEUF

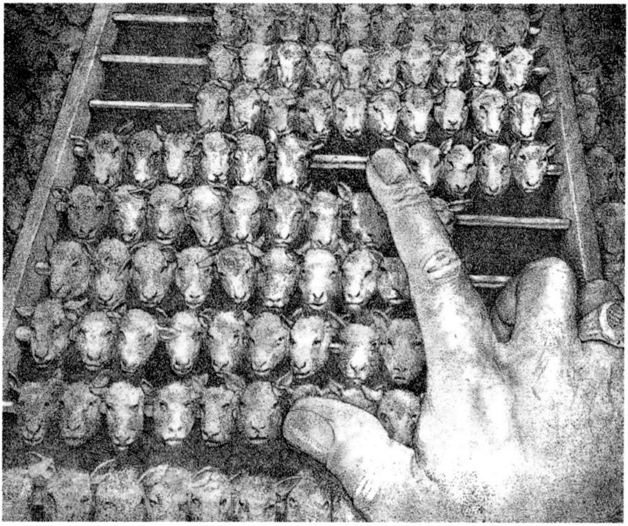

DAVID CHELSEA

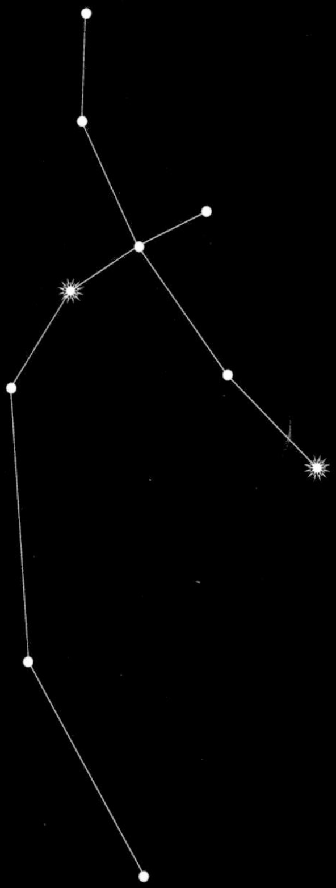

Perseus

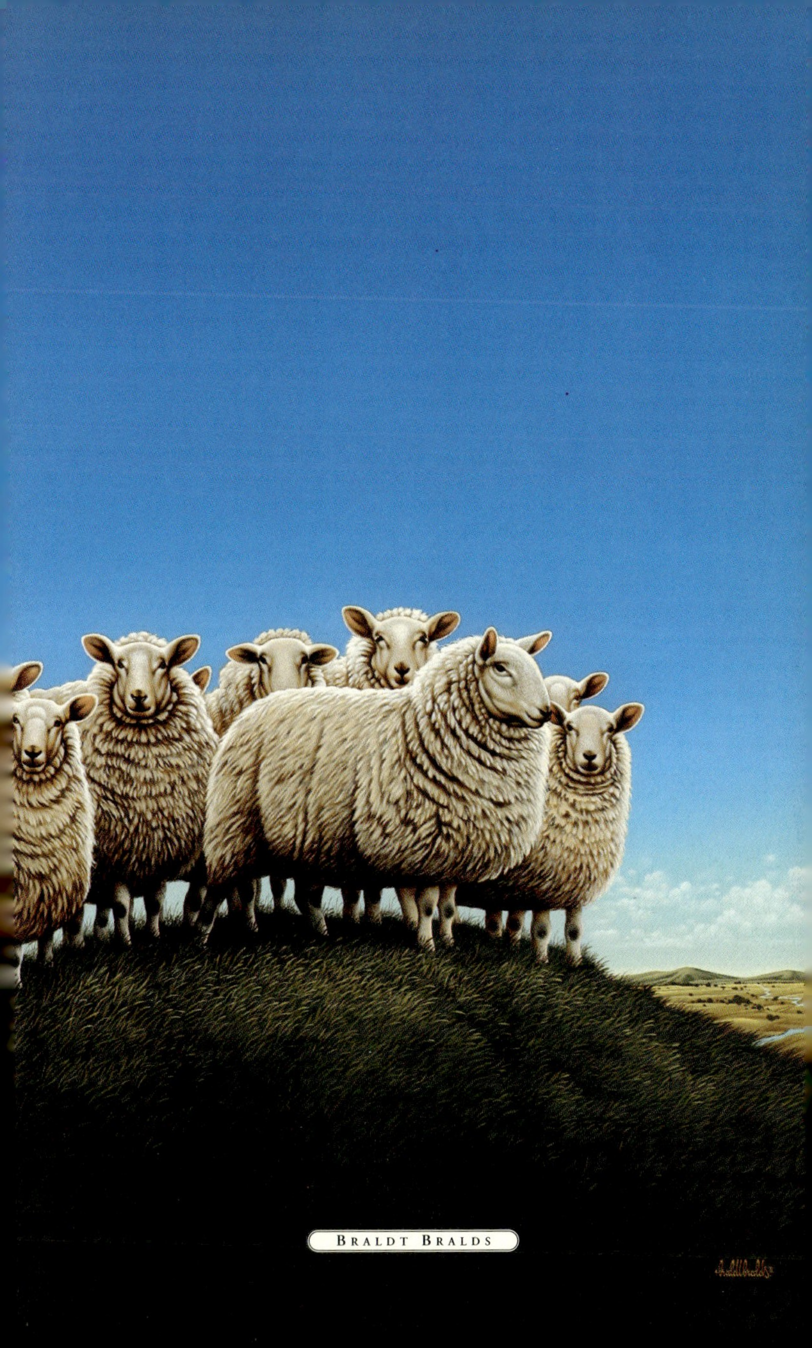
BRALDT BRALDS

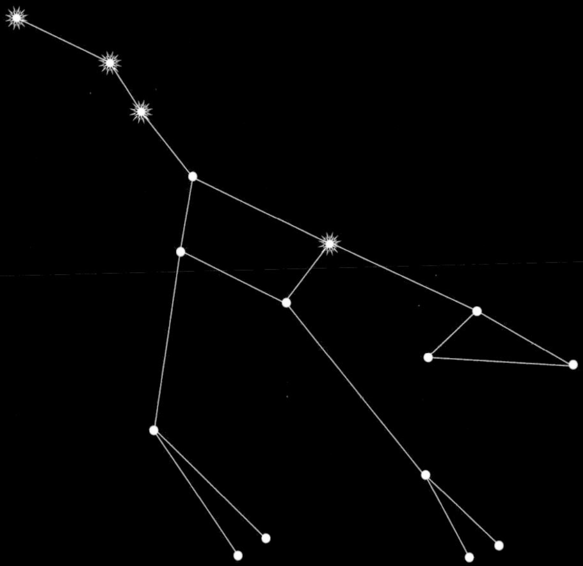

Ursa Major

23

TWENTY-THREE

DREIUNDZWANZIG

VINGT-TROIS

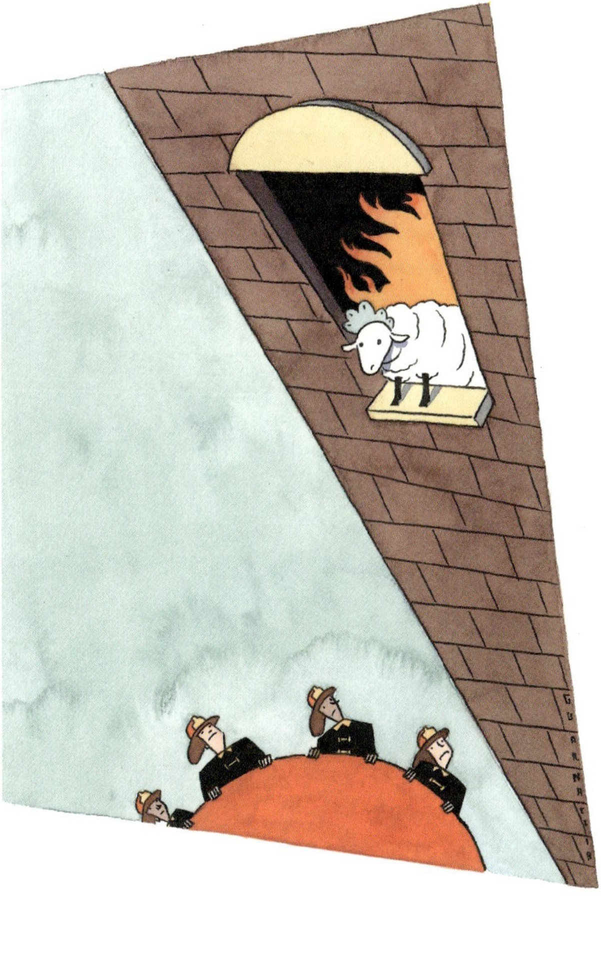

STEVEN GUARNACCIA

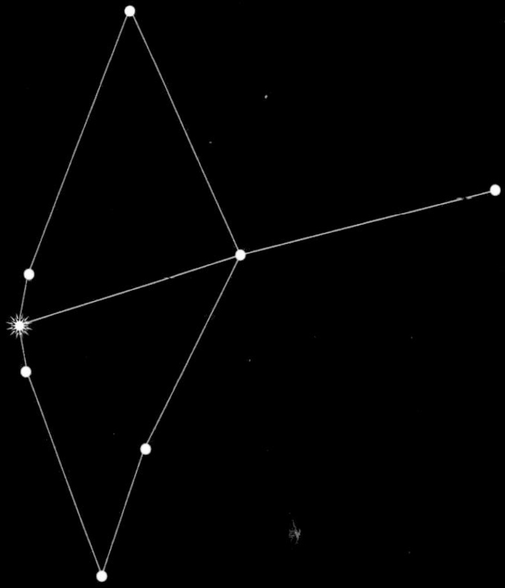

Acquila the Eagle

25

TWENTY-FIVE

FÜNFUNDZWANZIG

VINGT-CINQ

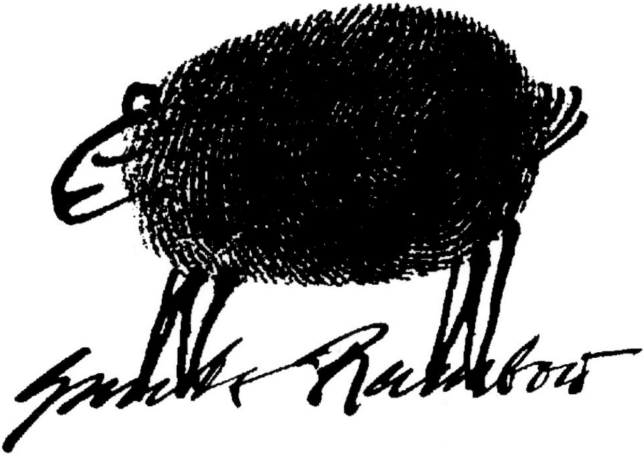

GUNTER RAMBOW

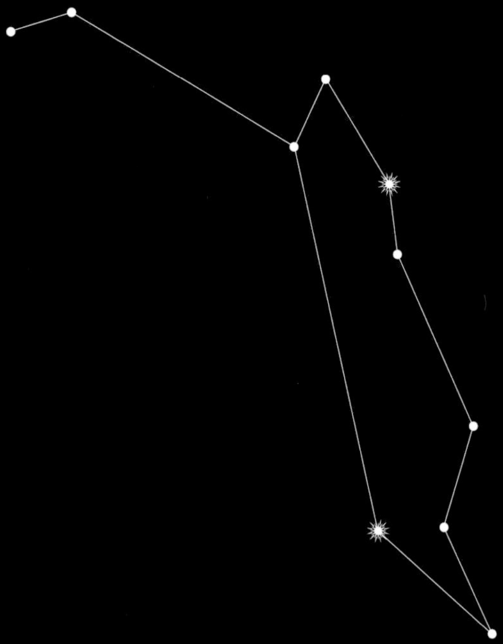

Sagittarius the Archer

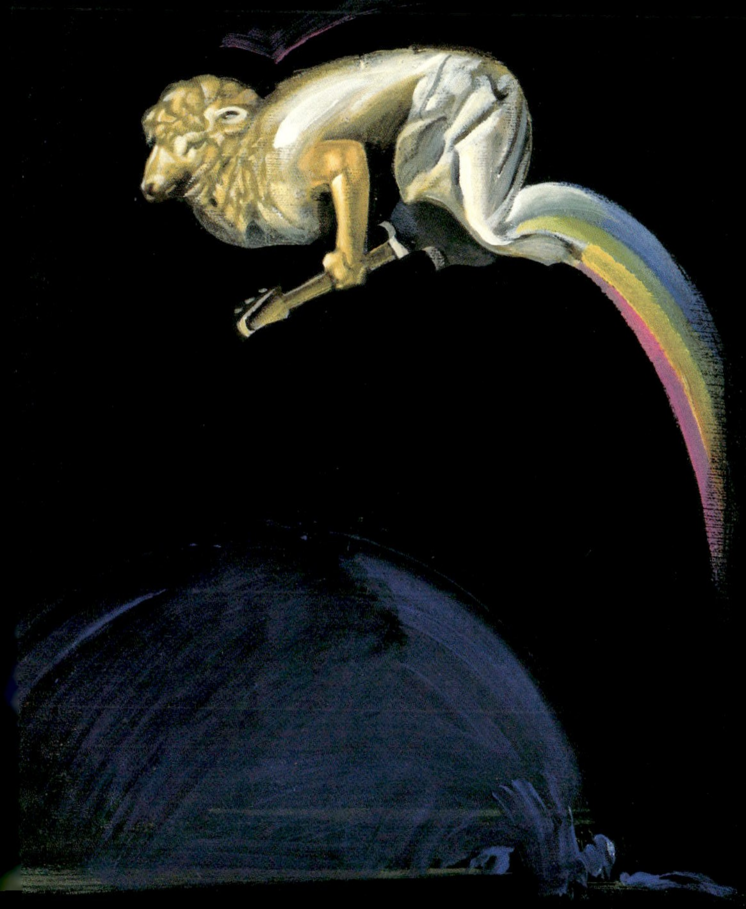

ABE ECHEVARRIA

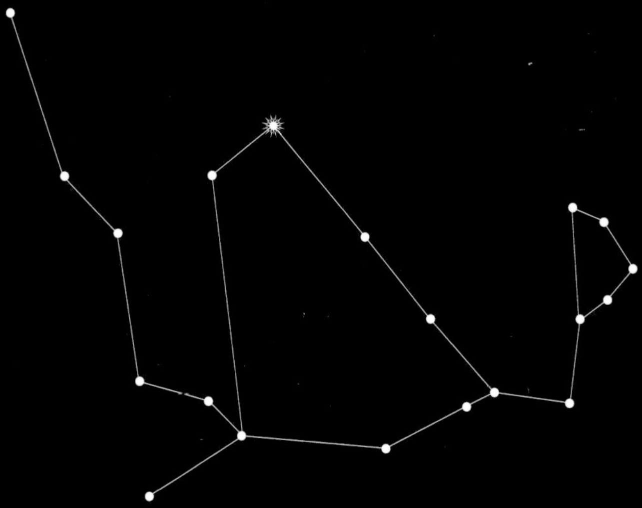

Ophiuchus the Serpent Bearer

29

TWENTY-NINE

NEUNUNDZWANZIG

VINGT-NEUF

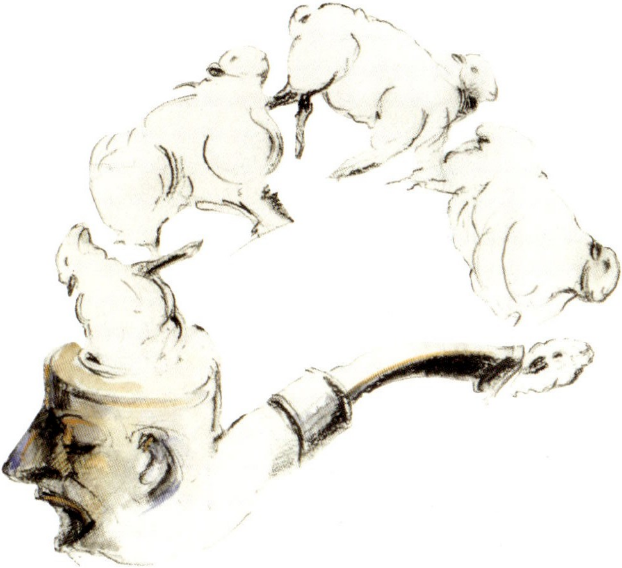

GEOFFREY MOSS

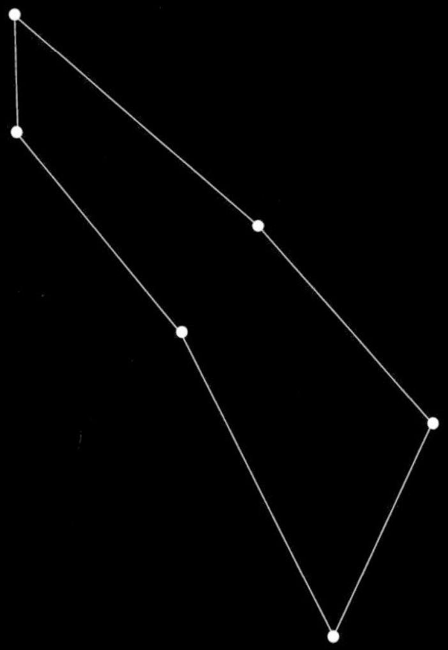

Lepus the Hare

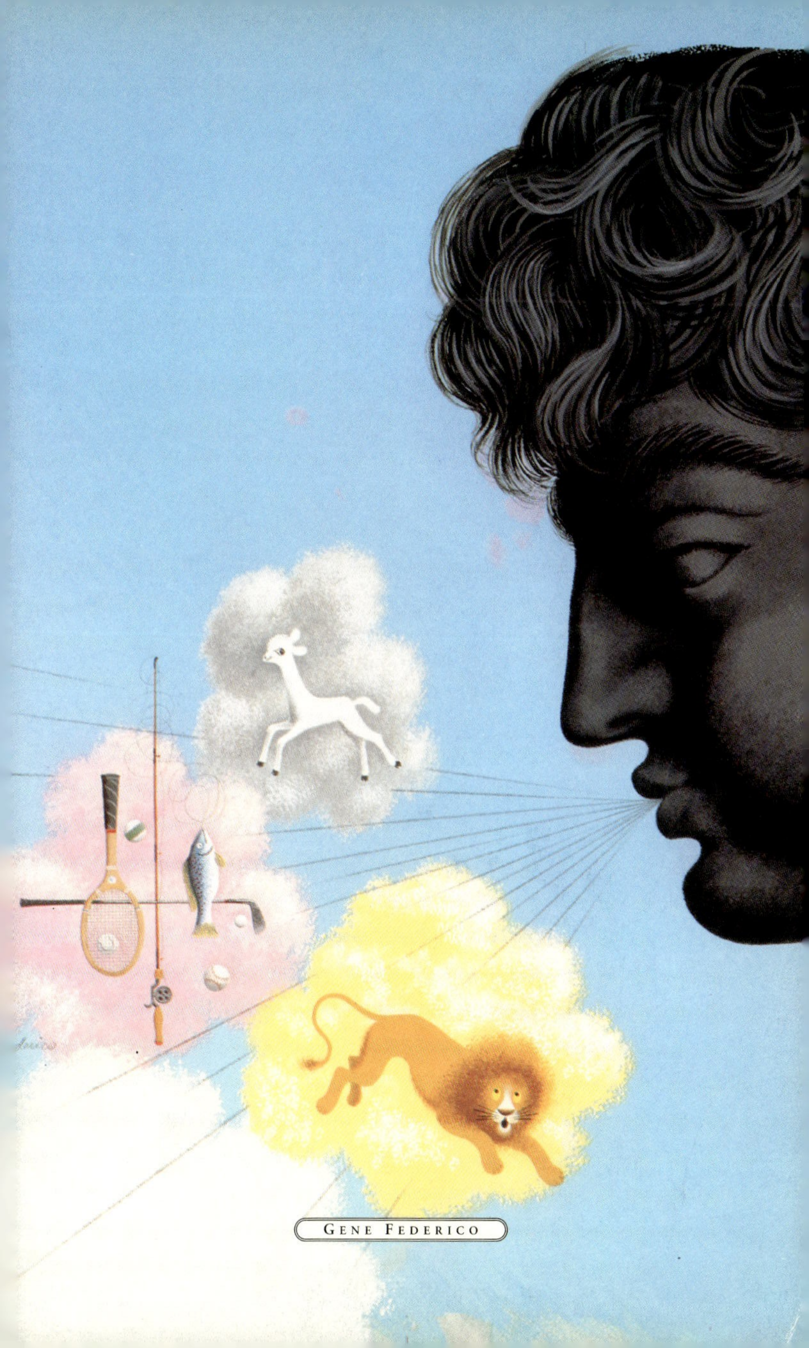
GENE FEDERICO

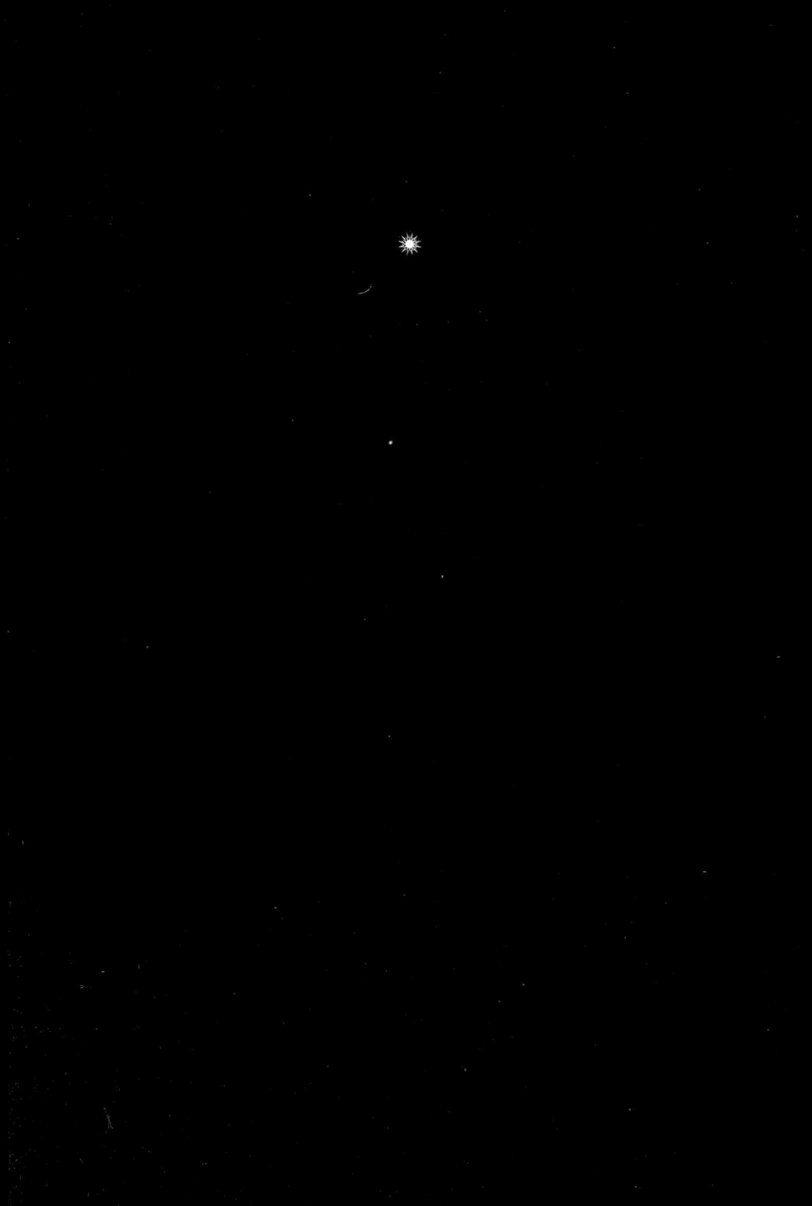

Polaris

33

THIRTY-THREE

DREIUNDDREISSIG

TRENTE-TROIS

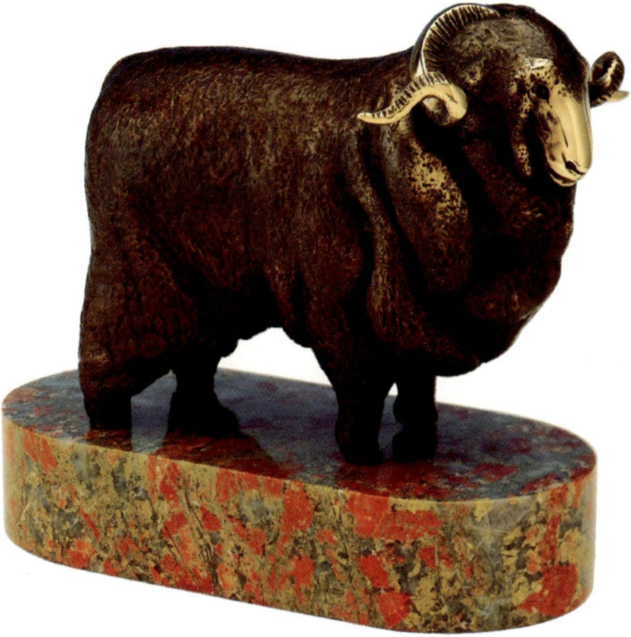

EDWARD J. BURKE

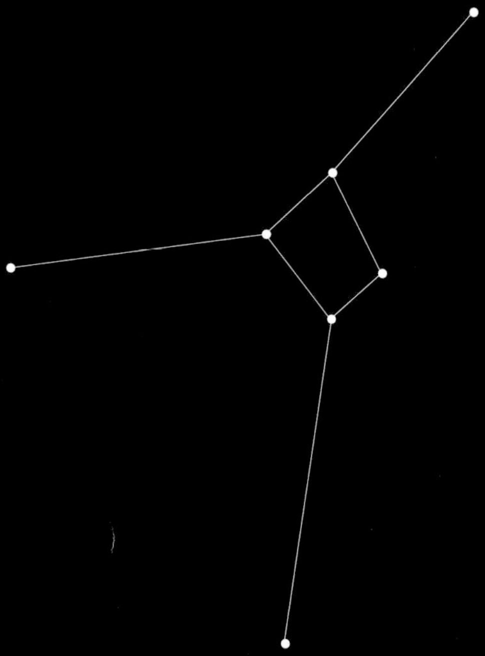

Cancer the Crab

35

THIRTY-FIVE

FÜNFUNDDREISSIG

TRENTE-CINQ

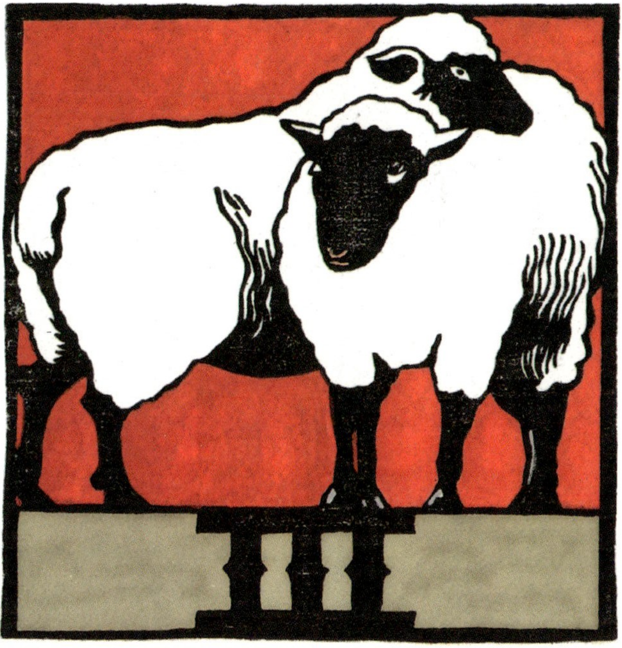

TWO MAN SAW

FRANCES CICHETTI, LARS HOKANSON

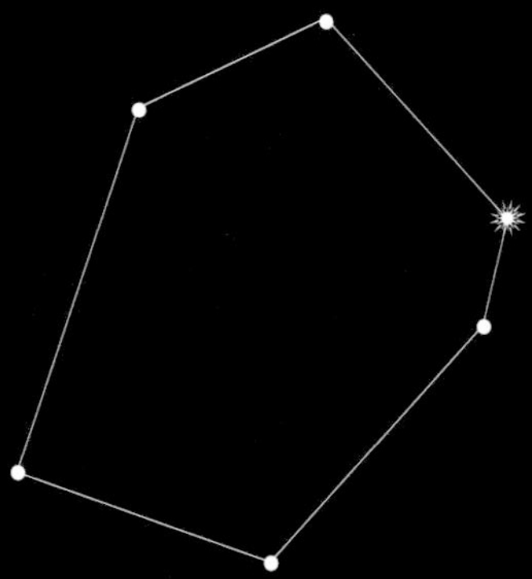

Auriga the Charioteer

37

THIRTY-SEVEN

SIEBENUNDDREISSIG

TRENTE-SEPT

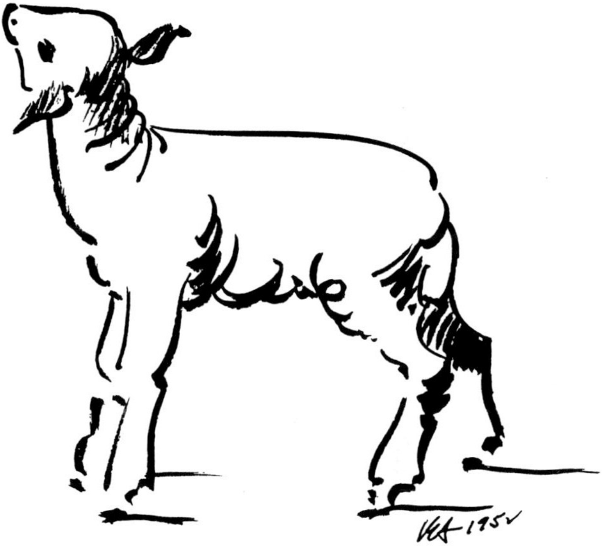

LEONARD EVERETT FISHER

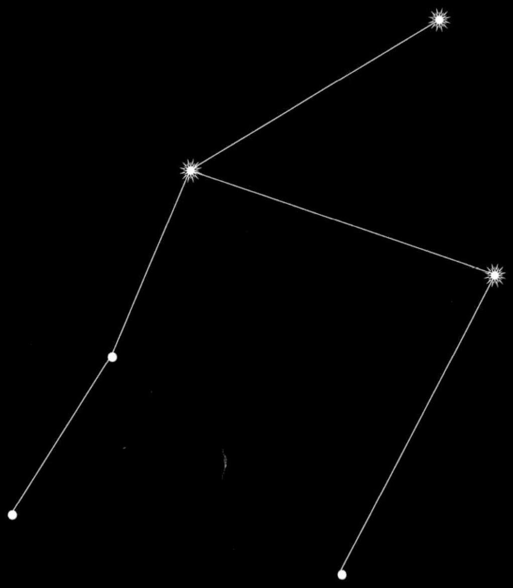

Libra the Scales

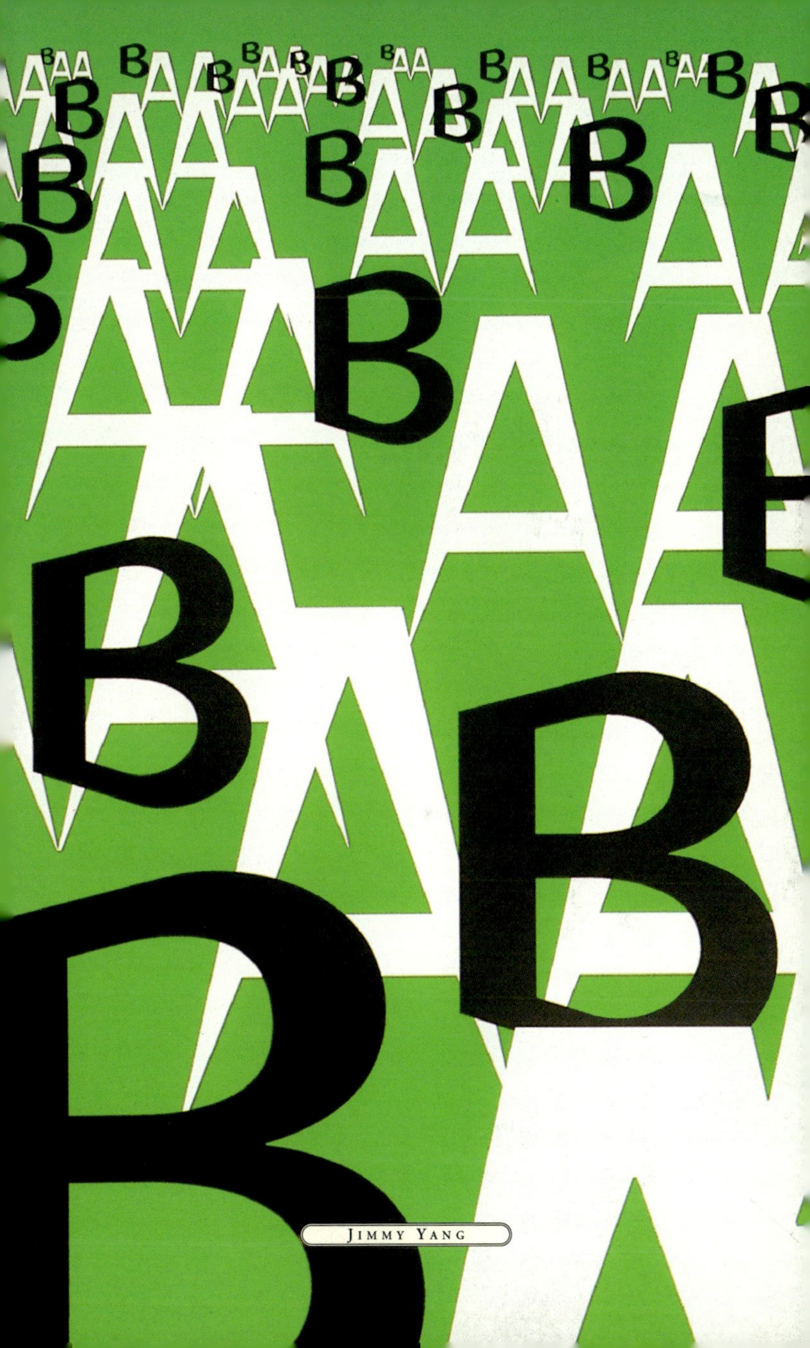
Jimmy Yang

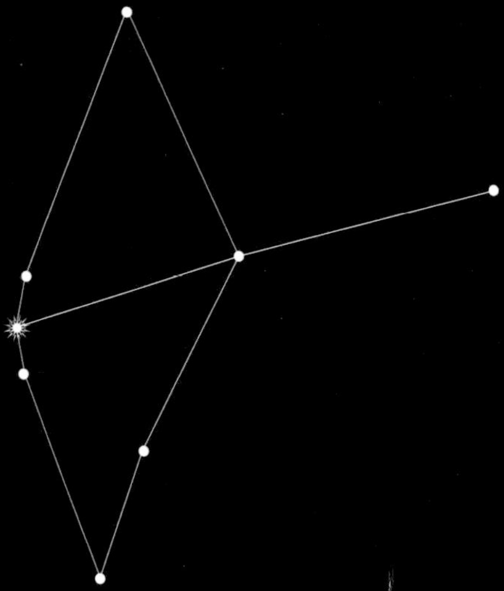

Acquila the Eagle

41

FORTY-ONE

EINUNDVIERZIG

QUARANTE ET UN

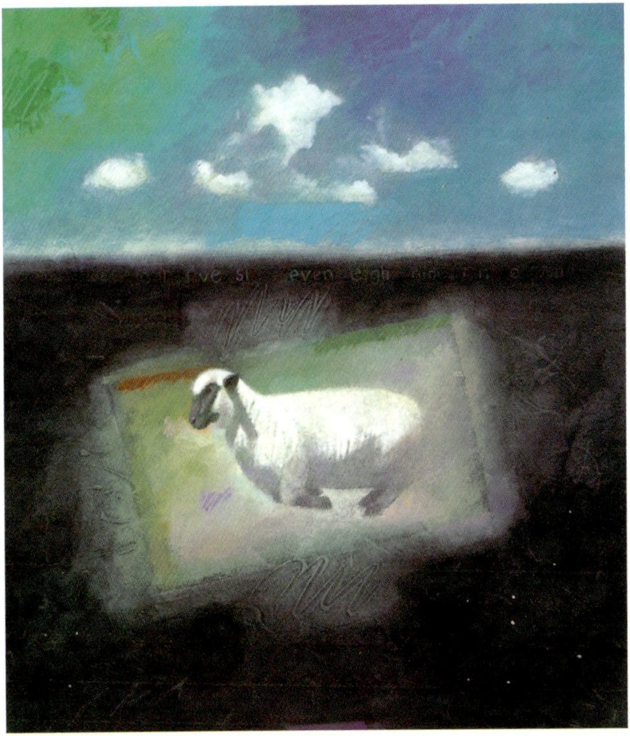

TERRY HOFF

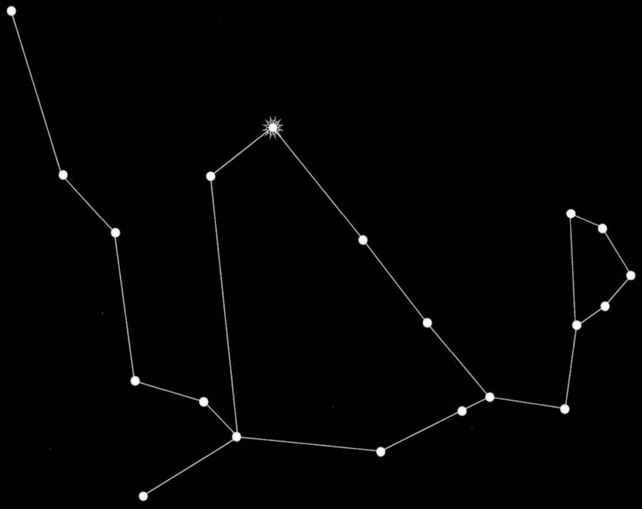

Ophiuchus the Serpent Bearer

43

FORTY-THREE

DREIUNDVIERZIG

QUARANTE-TROIS

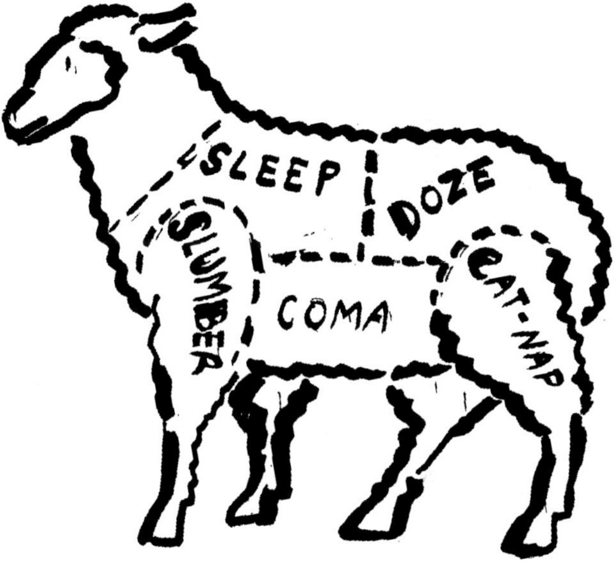

HEINZ EDELMANN

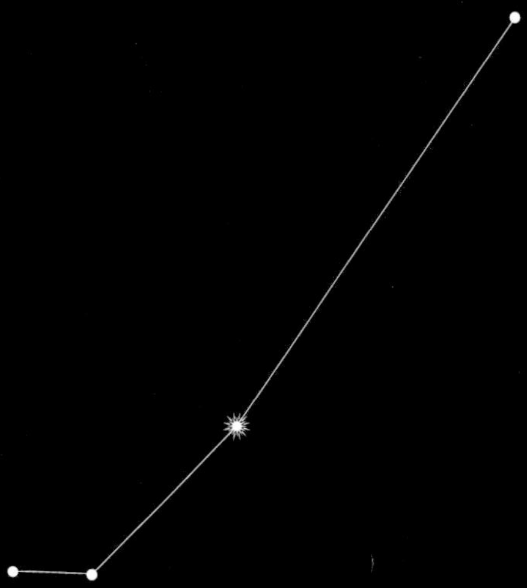

Aries

45

Forty-Five

Fünfundvierzig

Quarante-Cinq

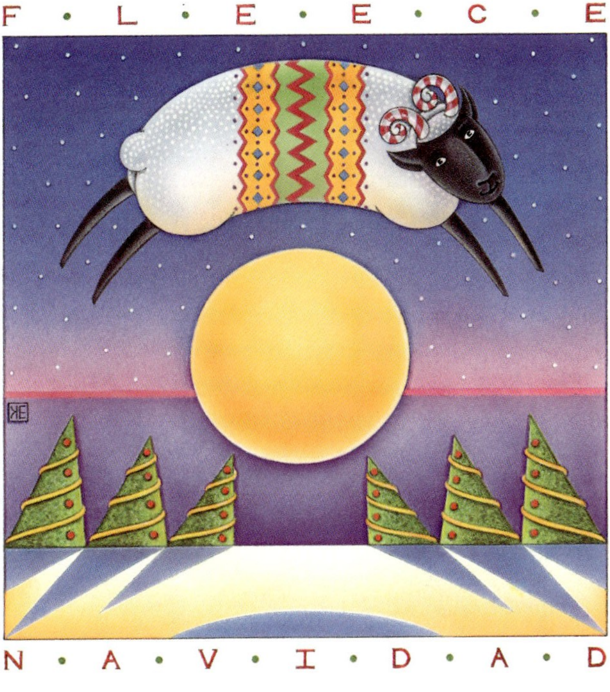

Kathi Ember

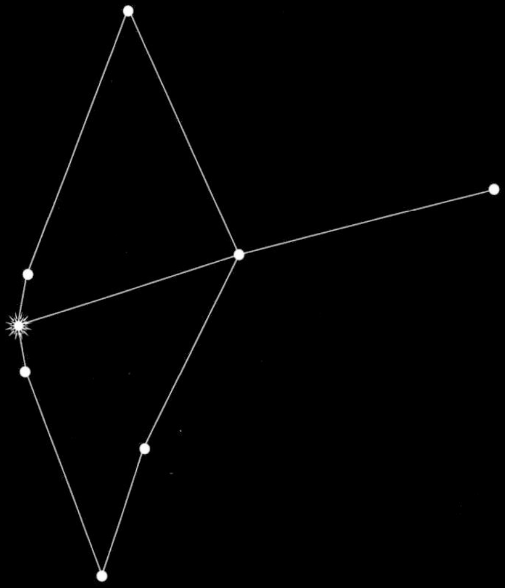

Acquila the Eagle

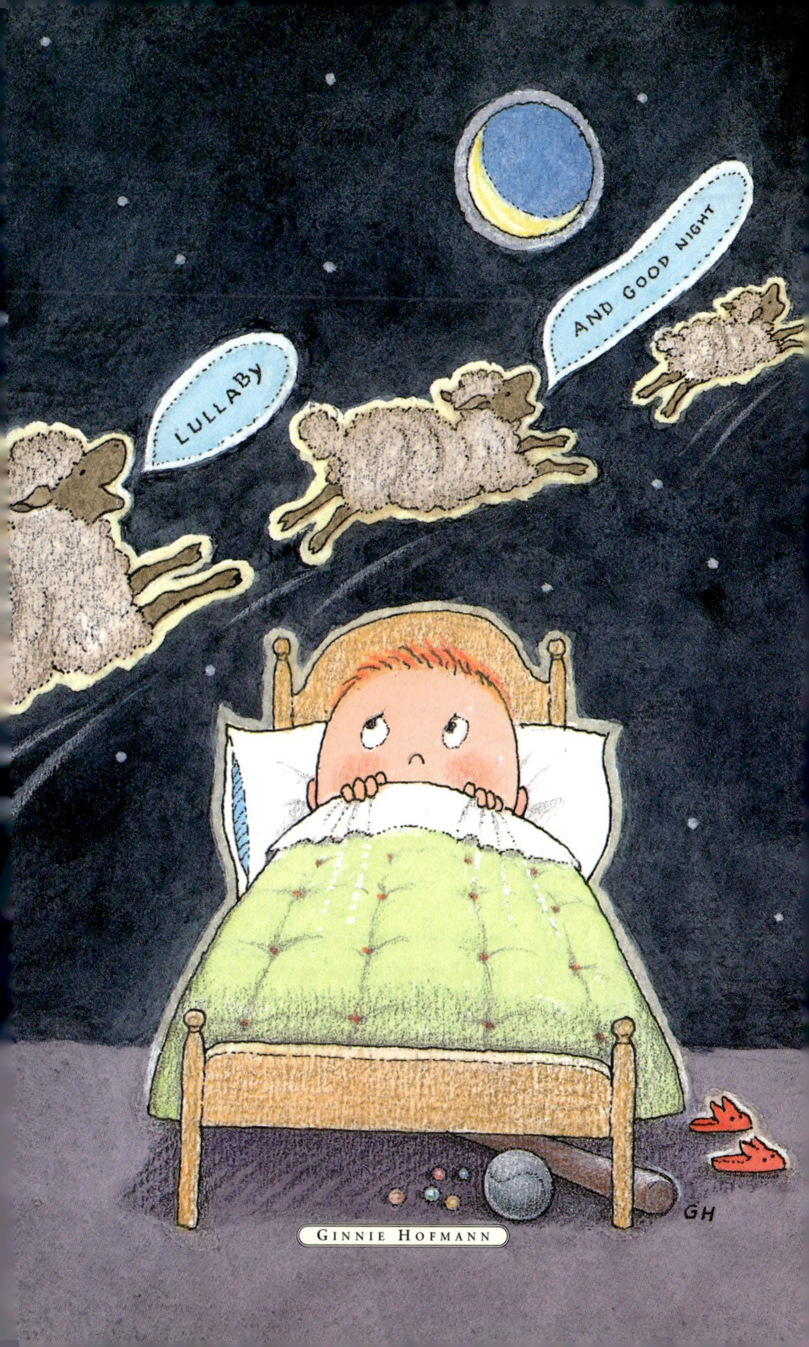
LULLABY
AND GOOD NIGHT
GH
GINNIE HOFMANN

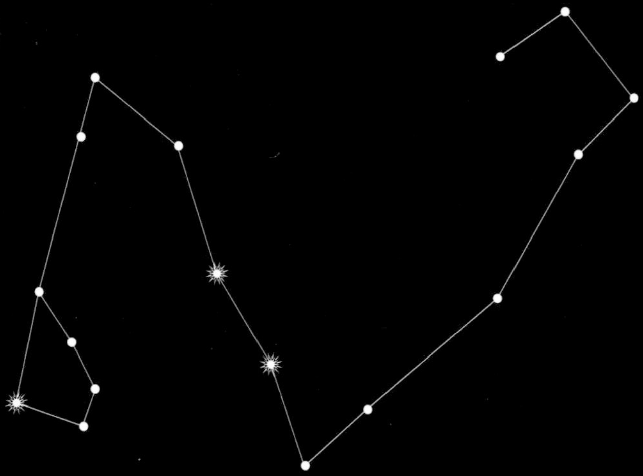

Draco the Dragon

49

FORTY-NINE

NEUNUNDVIERZIG

QUARANTE-NEUF

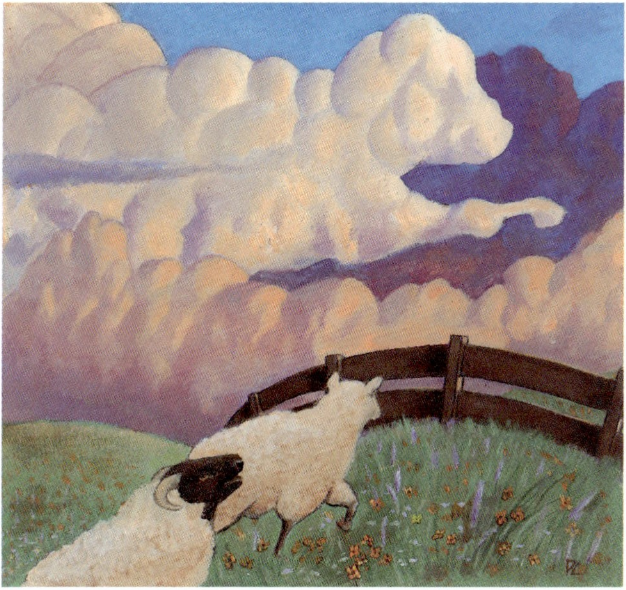

PATRICK CAMPBELL

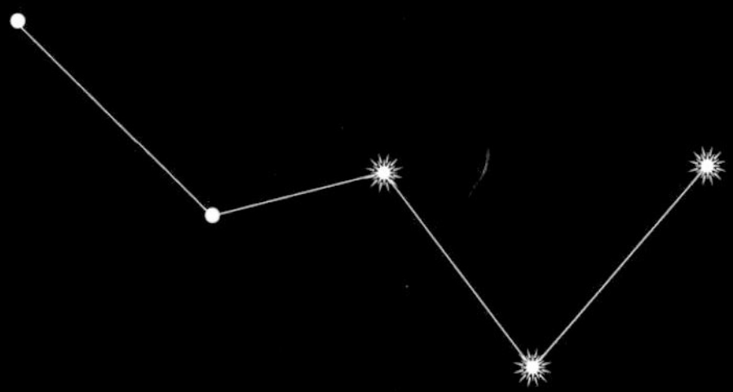

Cassopeia the Queen

51

FIFTY-ONE

EINUNDFÜNFZIG

CINQUANTE ET UN

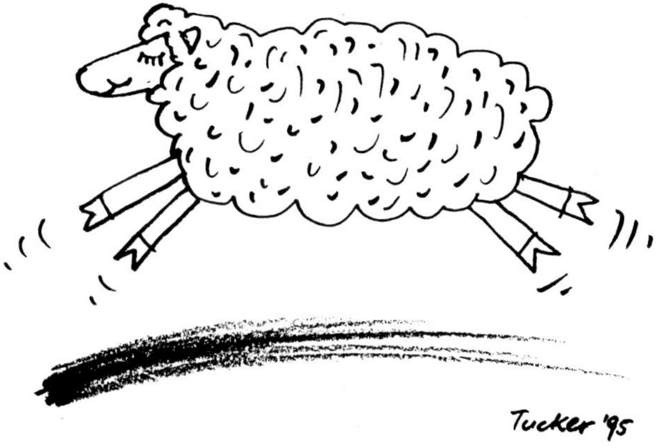

BARRIE TUCKER

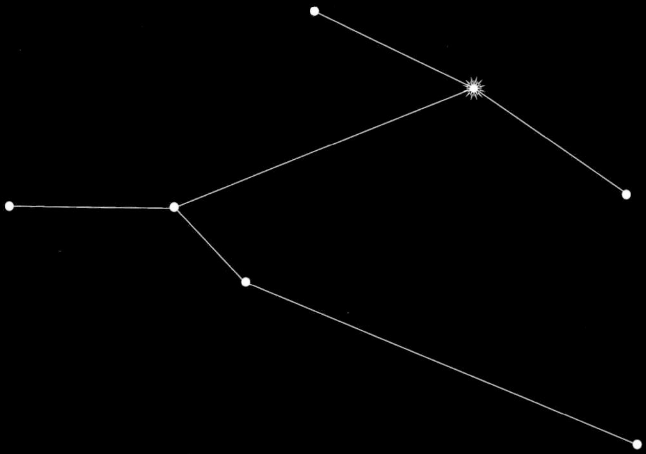

Canis Major

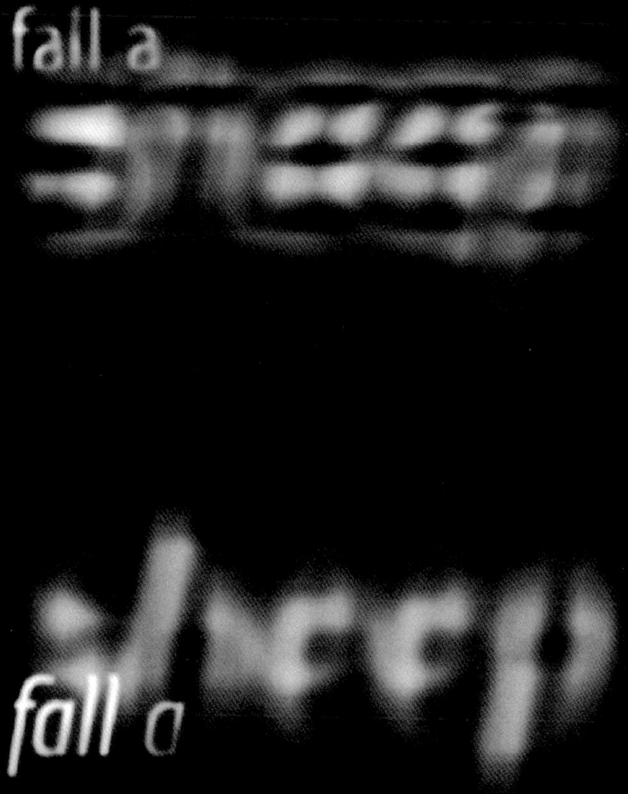

Simon Manchipp

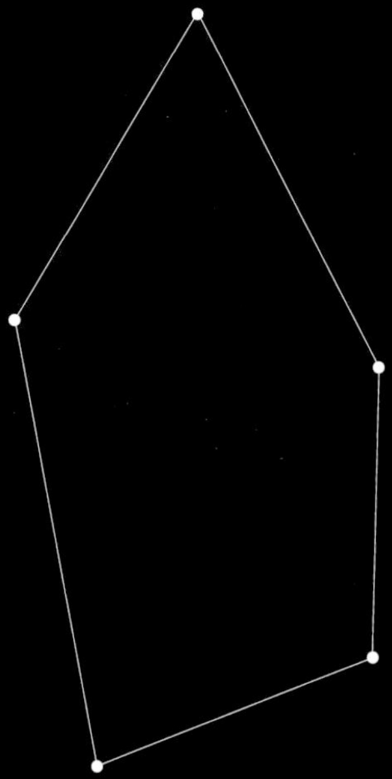

Cepheus the King

55

Fifty-Five

Fünfundfünfzig

Cinquante-Cinq

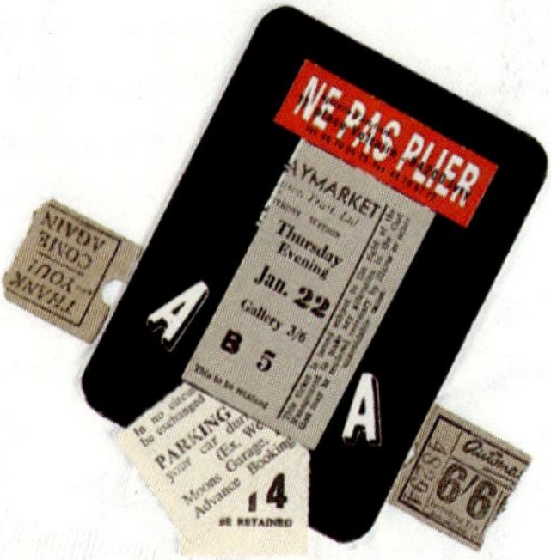

Alan Fletcher

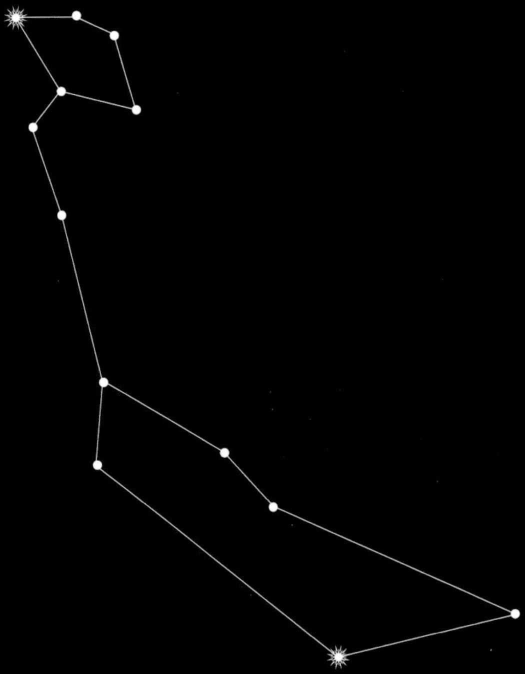

Cetus the Whale

57

FIFTY-SEVEN

SIEBENUNDFÜNFZIG

CINQUANTE-SEPT

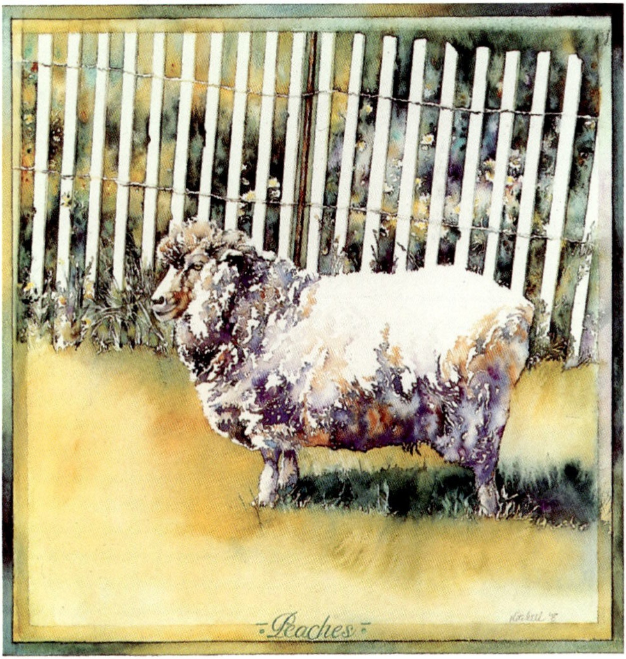

JOYCE KITCHELL

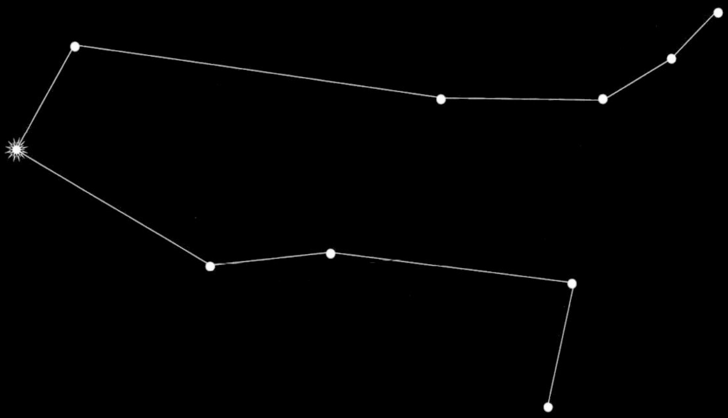

Gemini the Twins

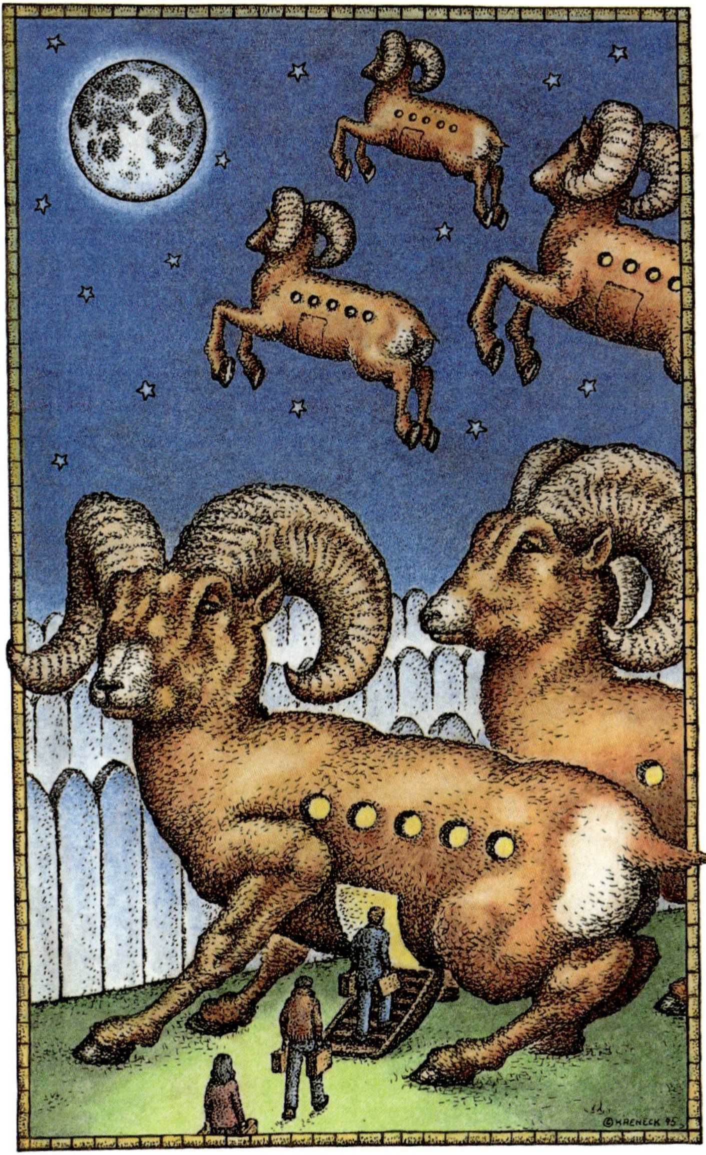

KEVIN KRENECK

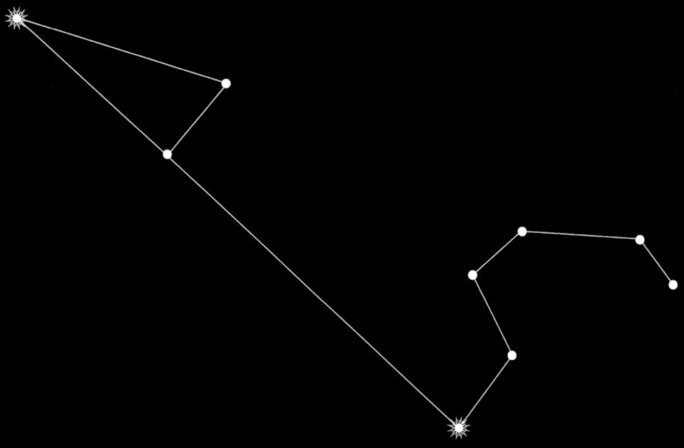

Leo the Lion

61

Sixty-One

Einundsechzig

Soixante Et Un

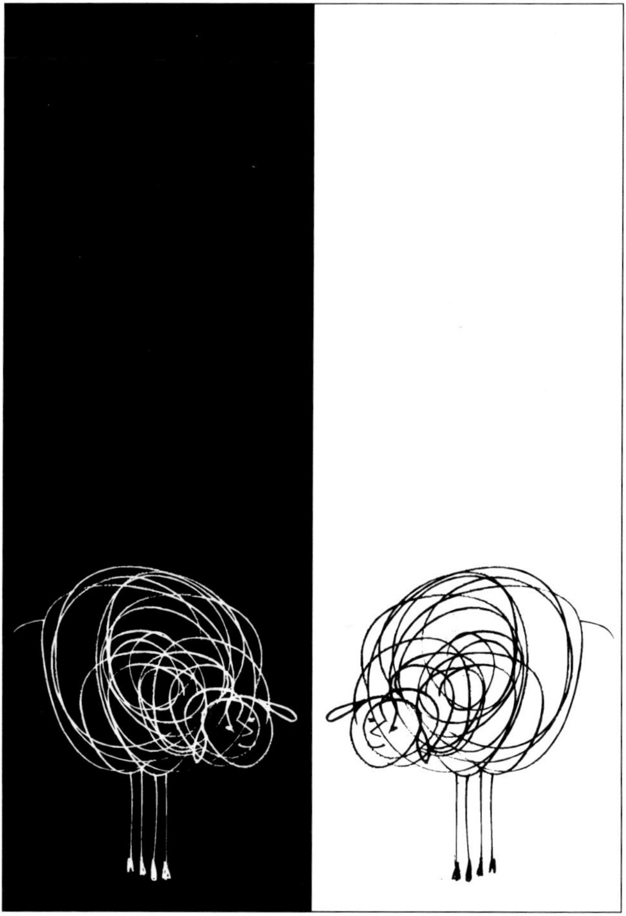

Dan Reisinger

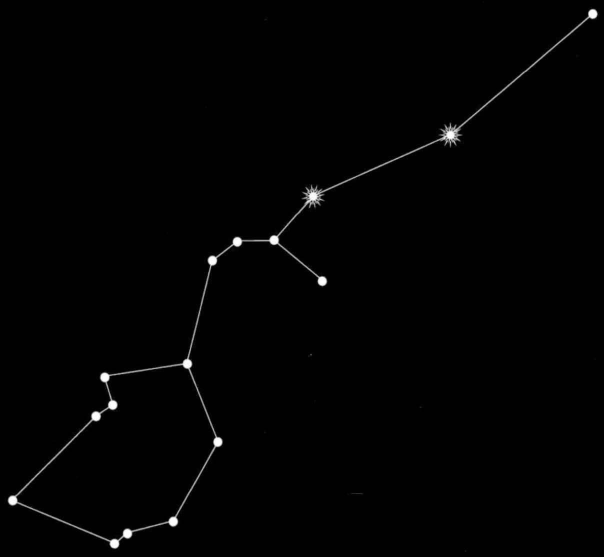

Aquarius

63

Sixty-Three
Dreiundsechzig
Soixante-Trois

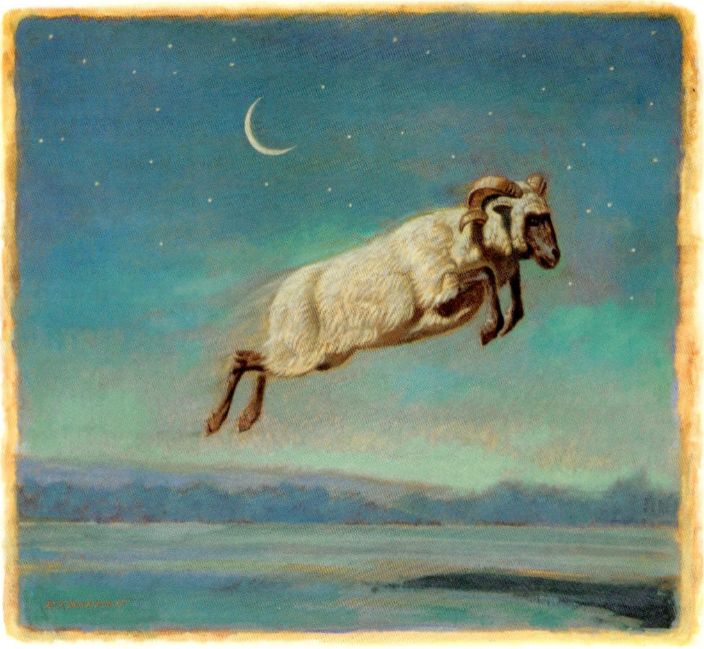

Robert Barrett

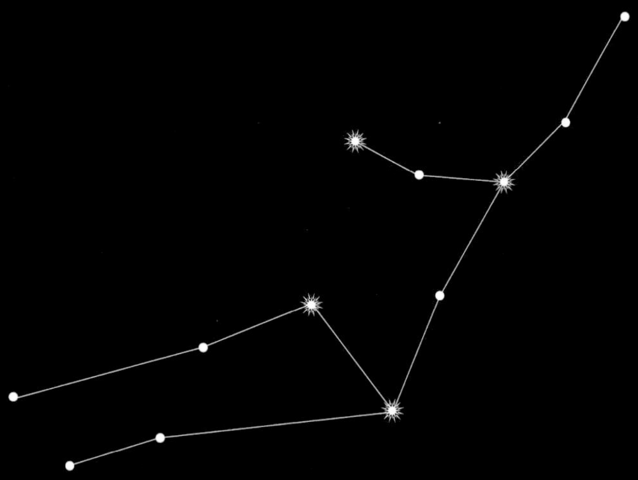

Virgo the Virgin

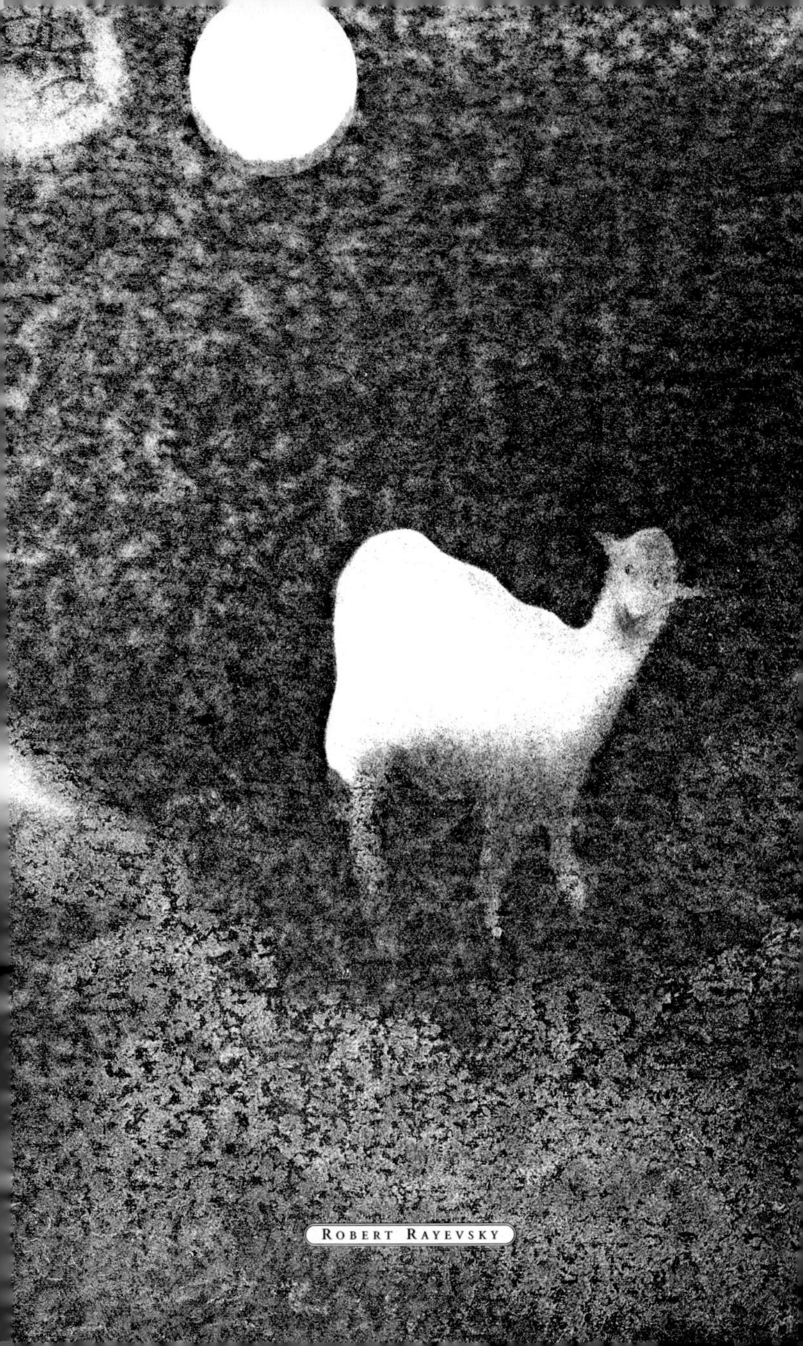
ROBERT RAYEVSKY

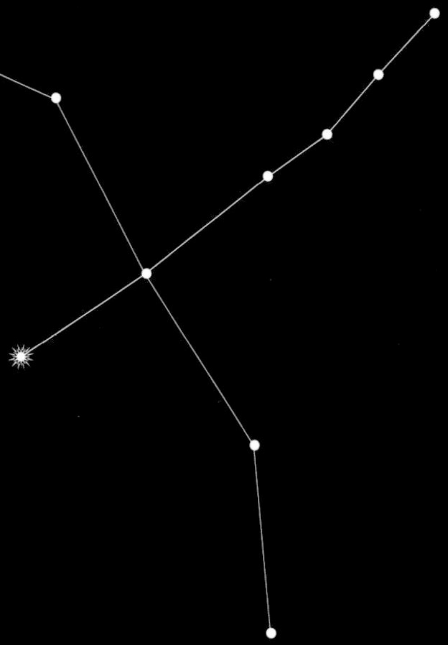

Cygnus the Swan

67

SIXTY-SEVEN

SIEBENUNDSECHZIG

SOIXANTE-SEPT

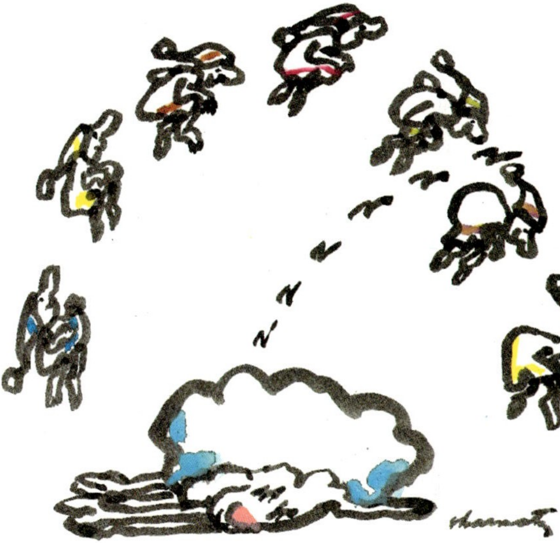

BILL CHARMATZ

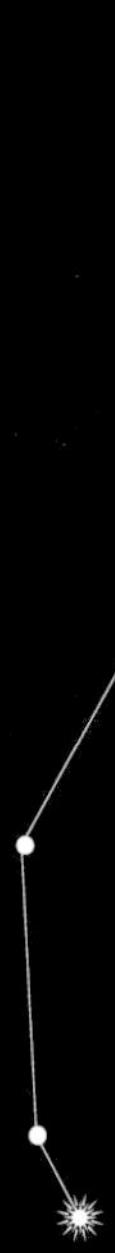

Lynx the Cat

69

SIXTY-NINE

NEUNUNDSECHZIG

SOIXANTE-NEUF

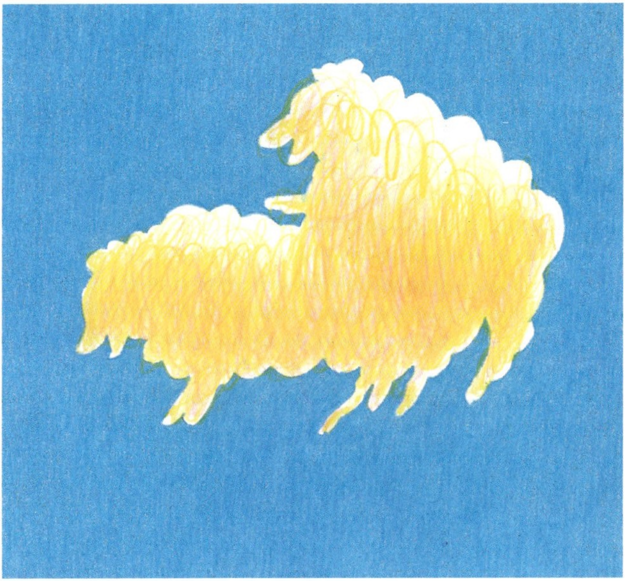

NIKLAUS TROXLER

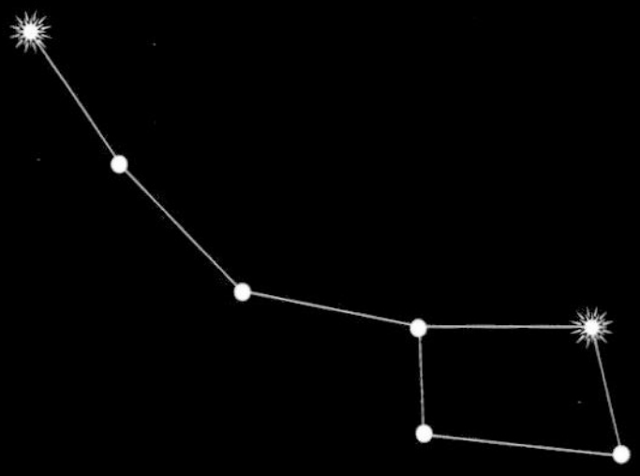

Ursa Monir

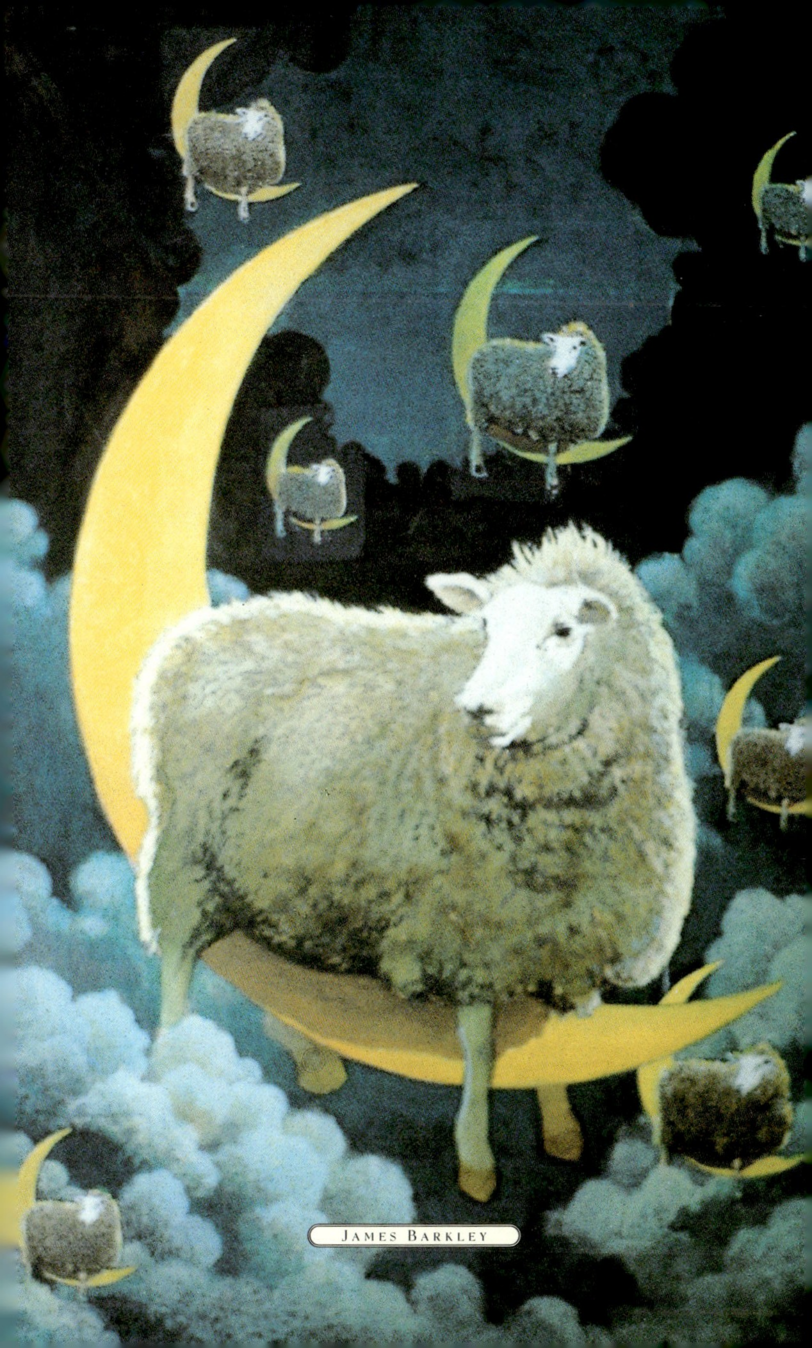
JAMES BARKLEY

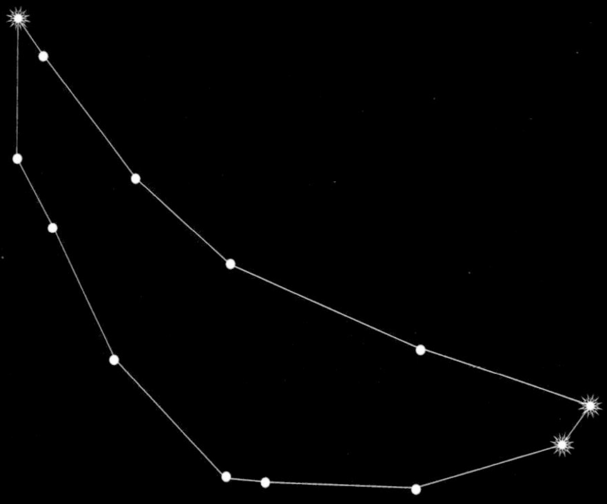

Capricornus

73

SEVENTY-THREE

DREISUNDSIEBZIG

SOIXANTE-TREIZE

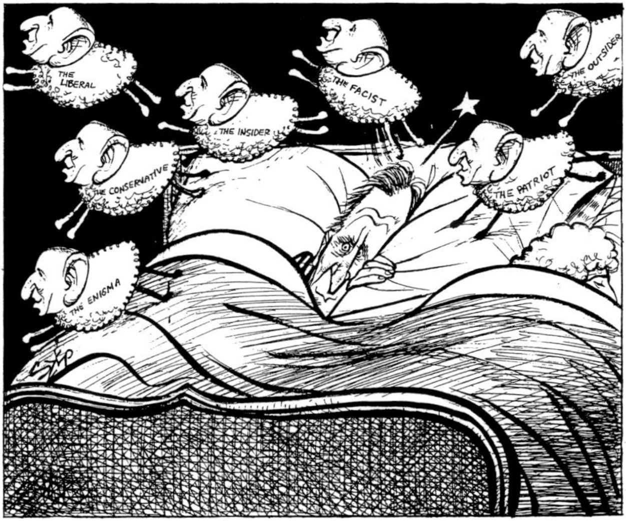

COUNTING PEROTS

PAUL SZEP

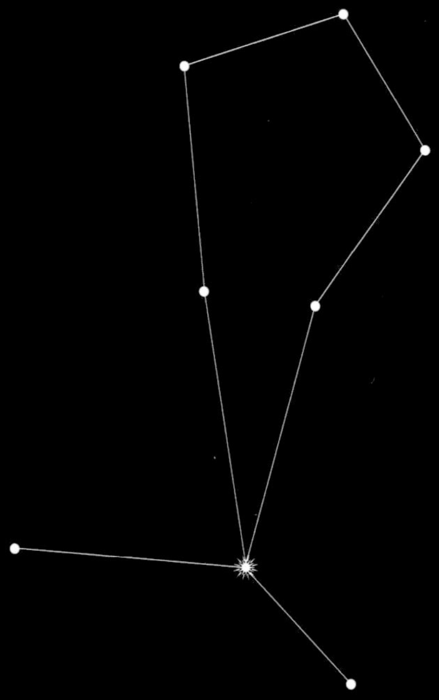

Bootes the Herdsman

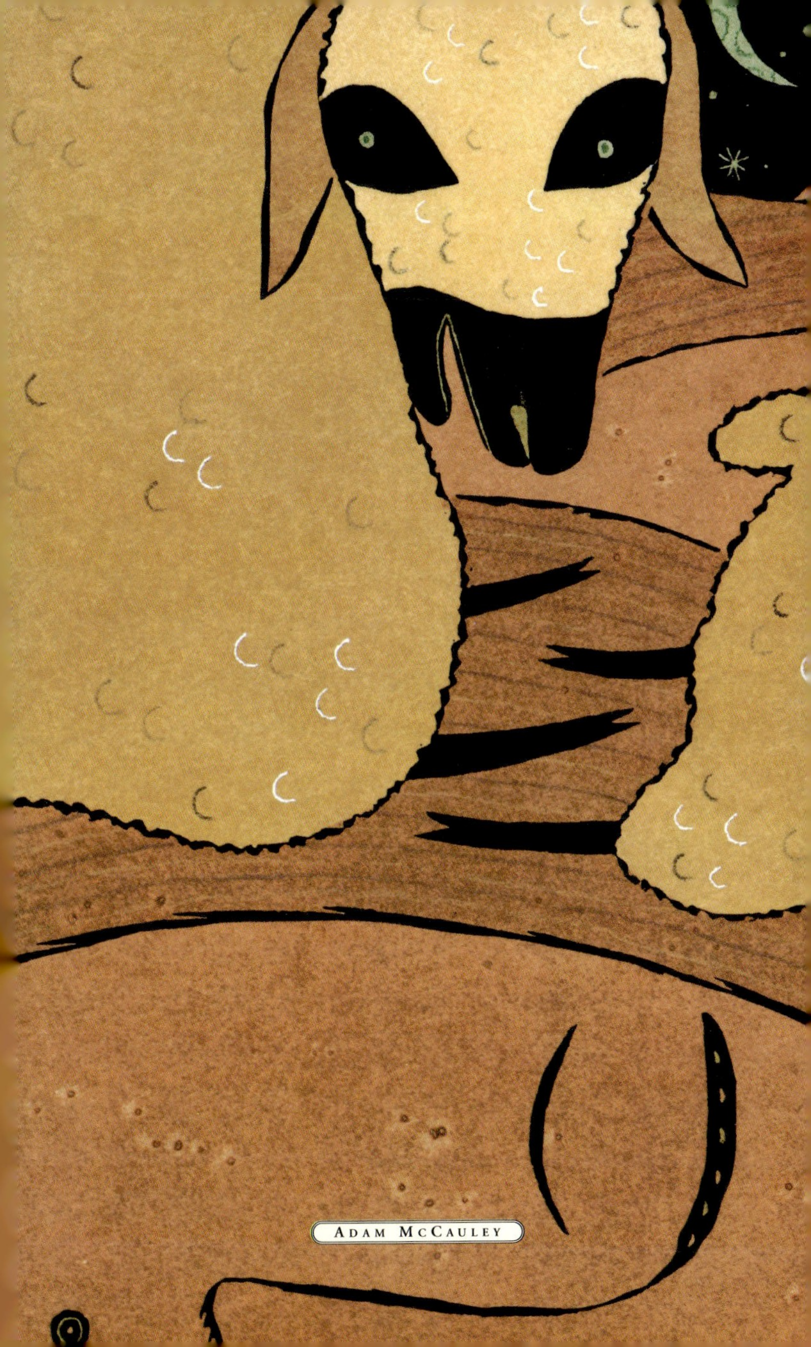
ADAM McCAULEY

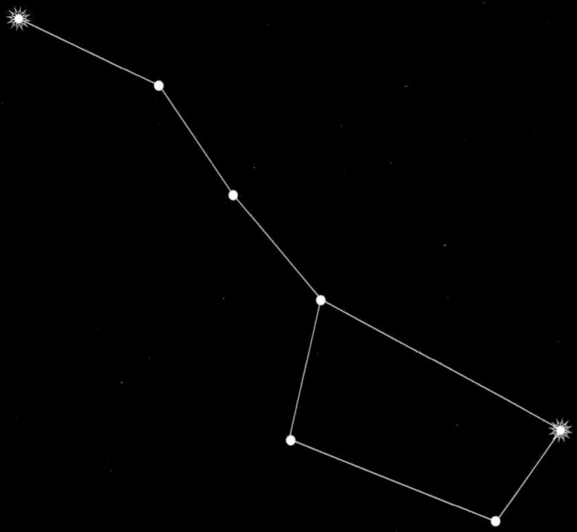

Big Dipper

77

SEVENTY-SEVEN

SIEBENUNDSIEBZIG

SOIXANTE-DIX-SEPT

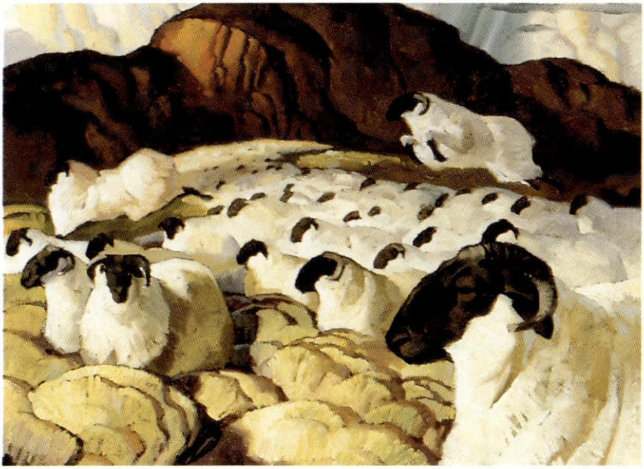

GREGORY MANCHESS

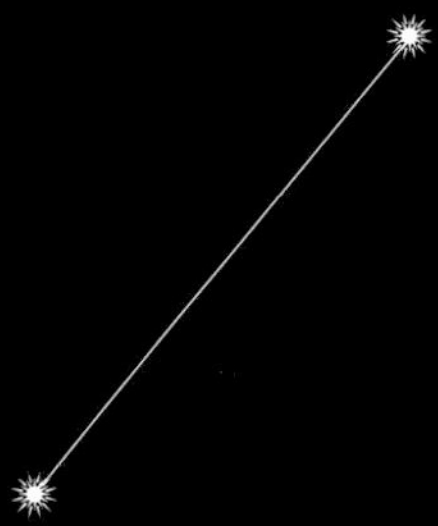

Canes Venatici

79

SEVENTY-NINE

NEUNUNDSIEBZIG

SOIXANTE-DIX-NEUF

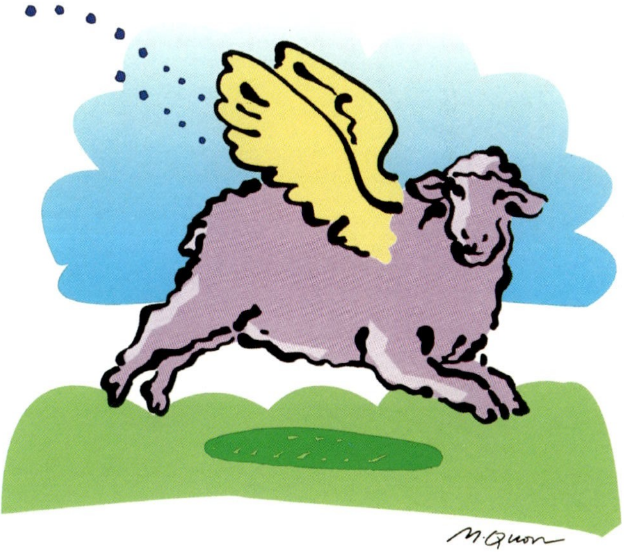

MIKE QUON

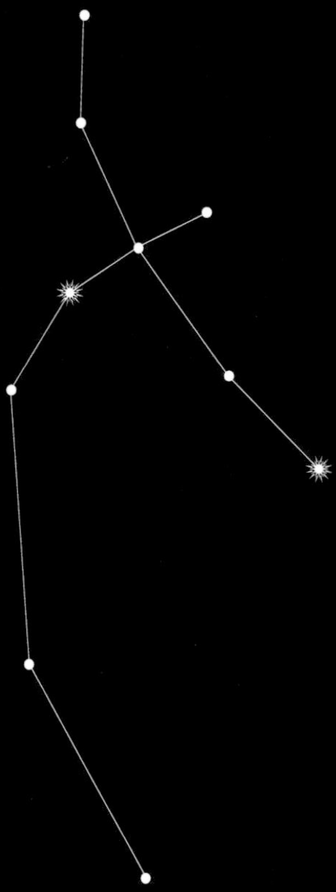

Perseus

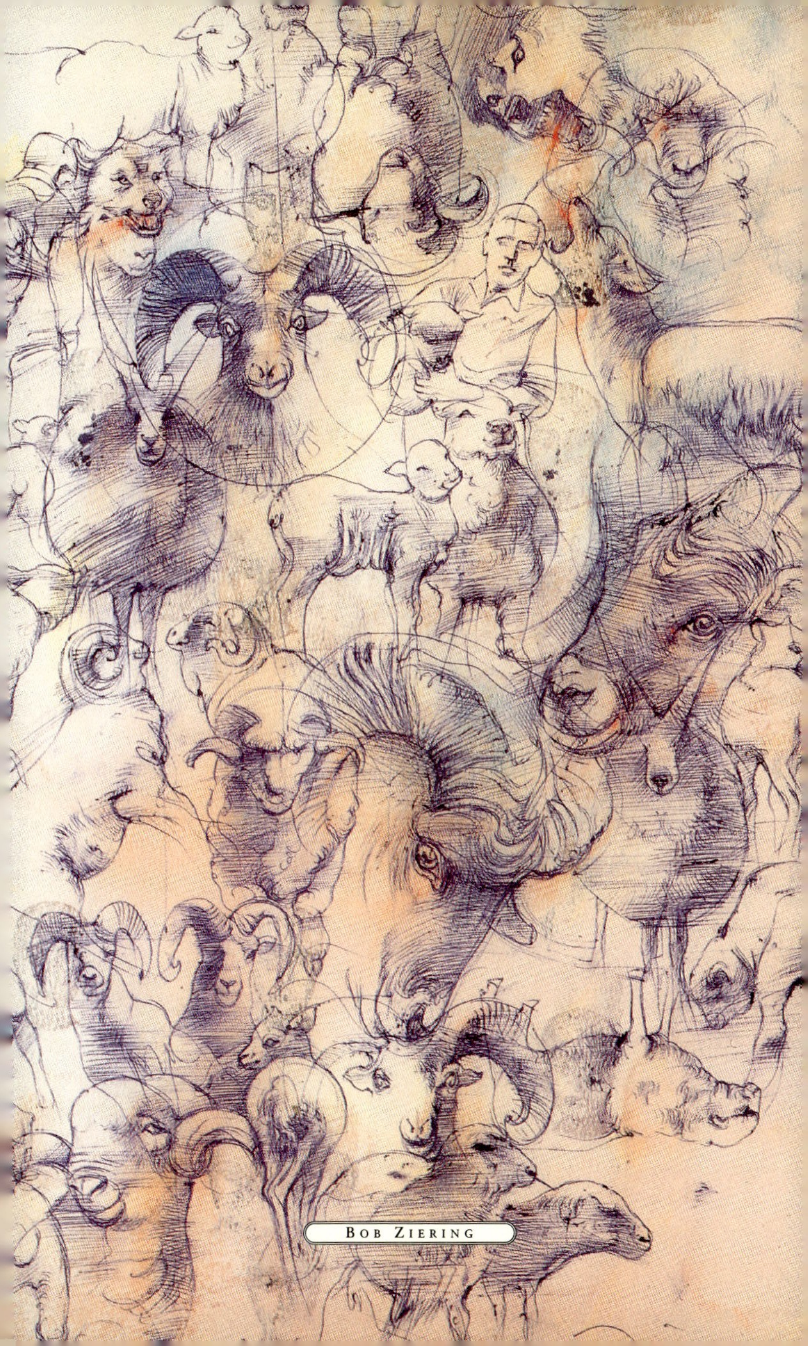

Bob Ziering

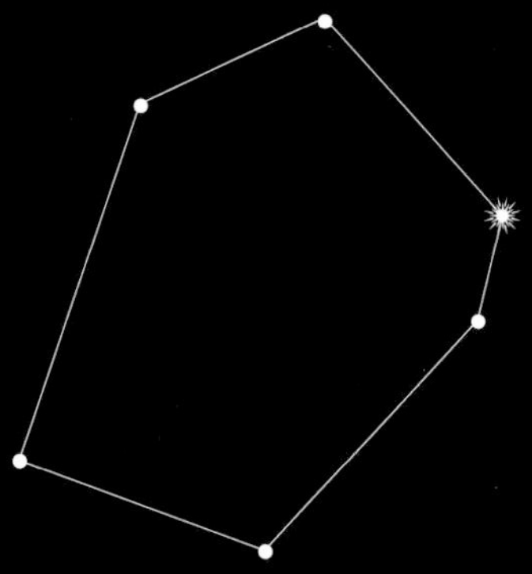

Auriga the Charioteer

83

Eighty-Three

Dreiundachtzig

Quatre-Vingt-Trois

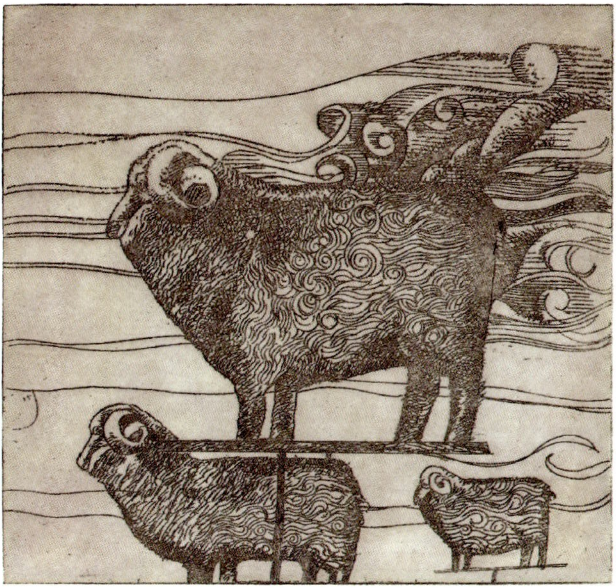

Ed Abrams

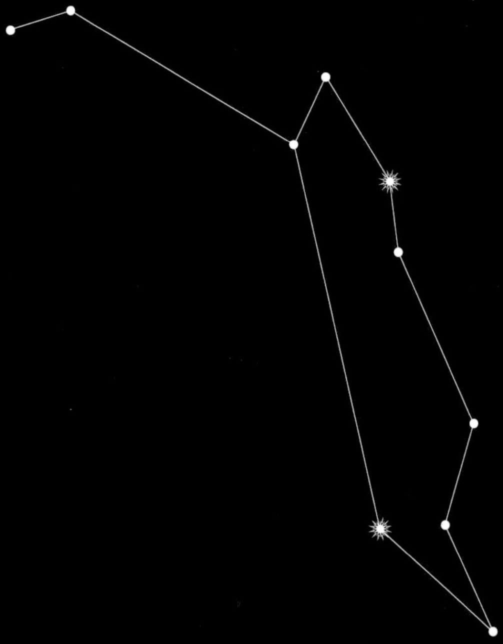

Sagittarius the Archer

85

EIGHTY-FIVE

FÜNFUNDACHTZIG

QUATRE-VINGT-CINQ

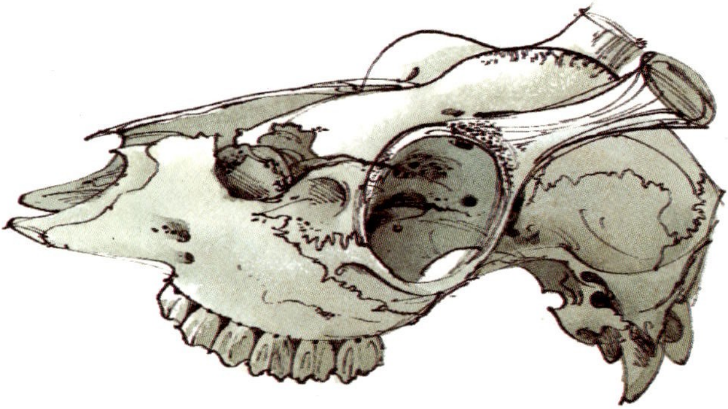

DAVID GENTLEMAN

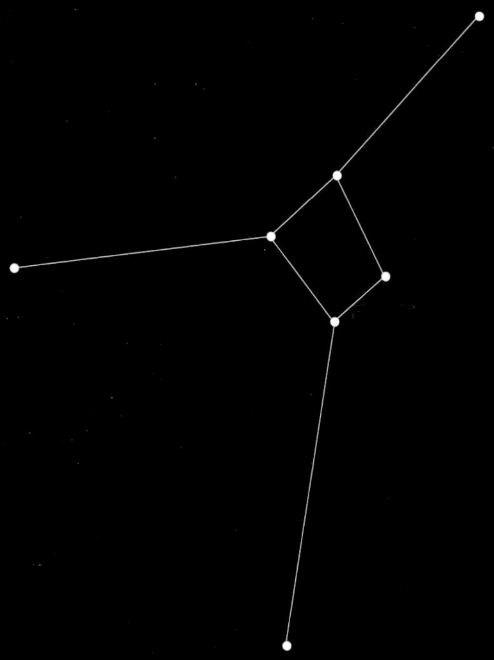

Cancer the Crab

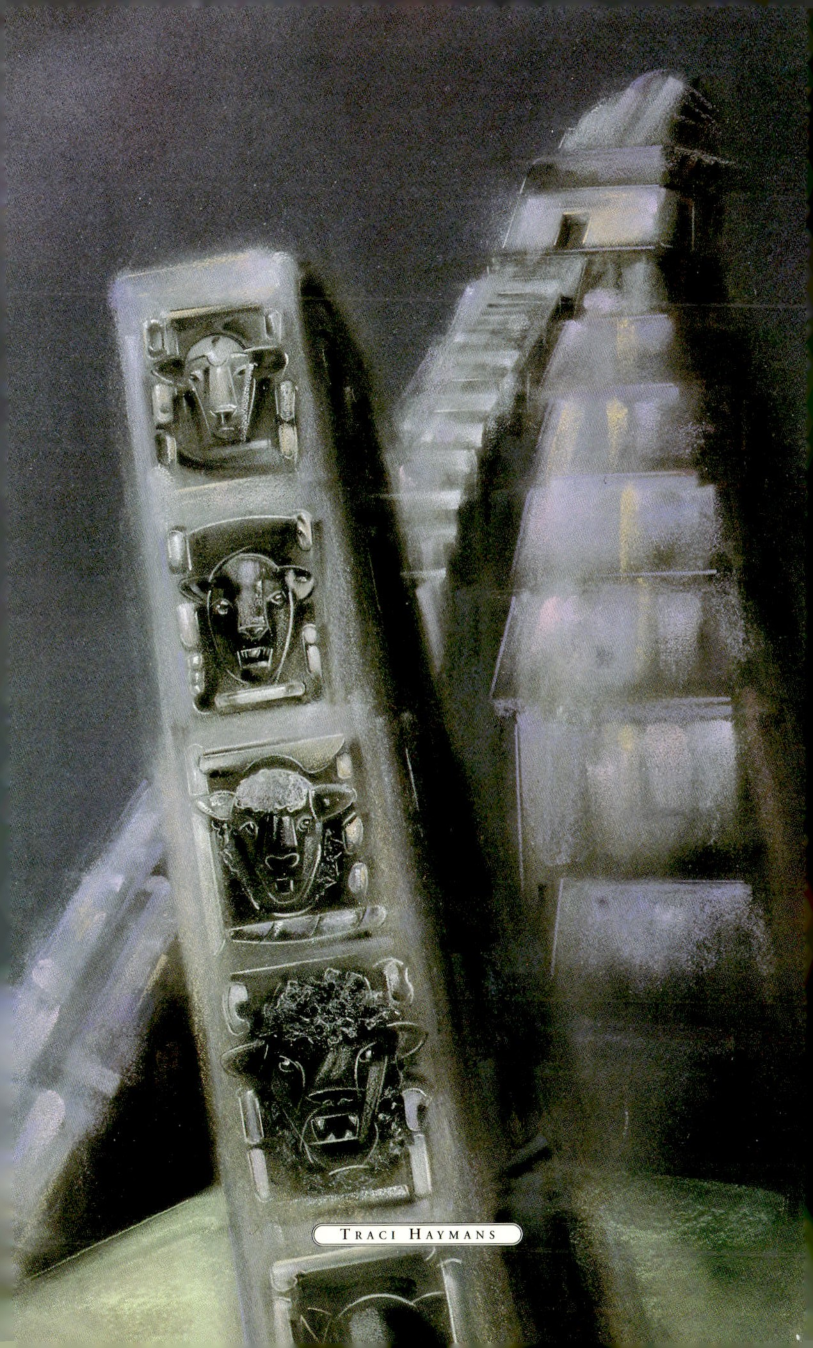

Traci Haymans

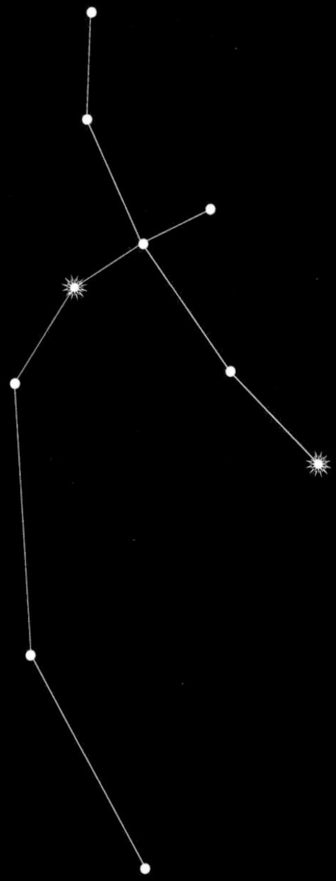

Perseus

89

EIGHTY-NINE

NEUNUNDACHTZIG

QUATRE-VINGT-NEUF

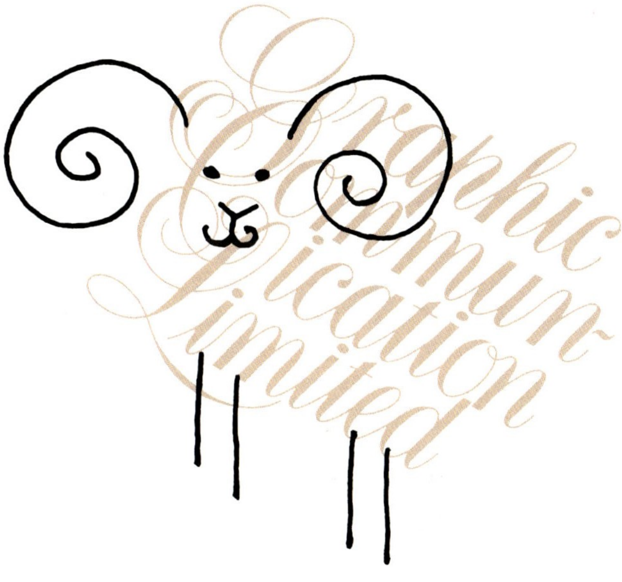

HENRY STEINER

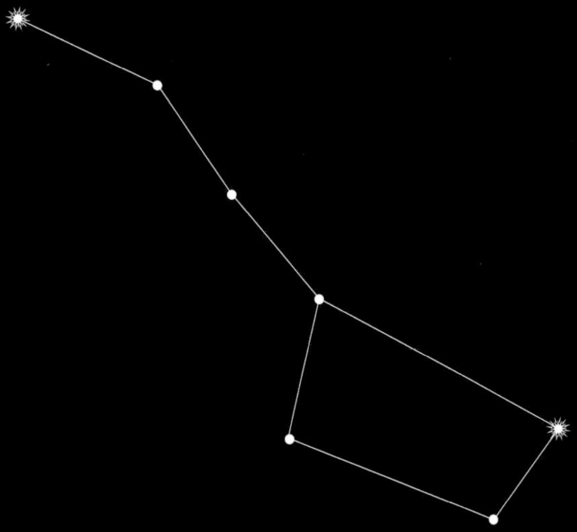

Big Dipper

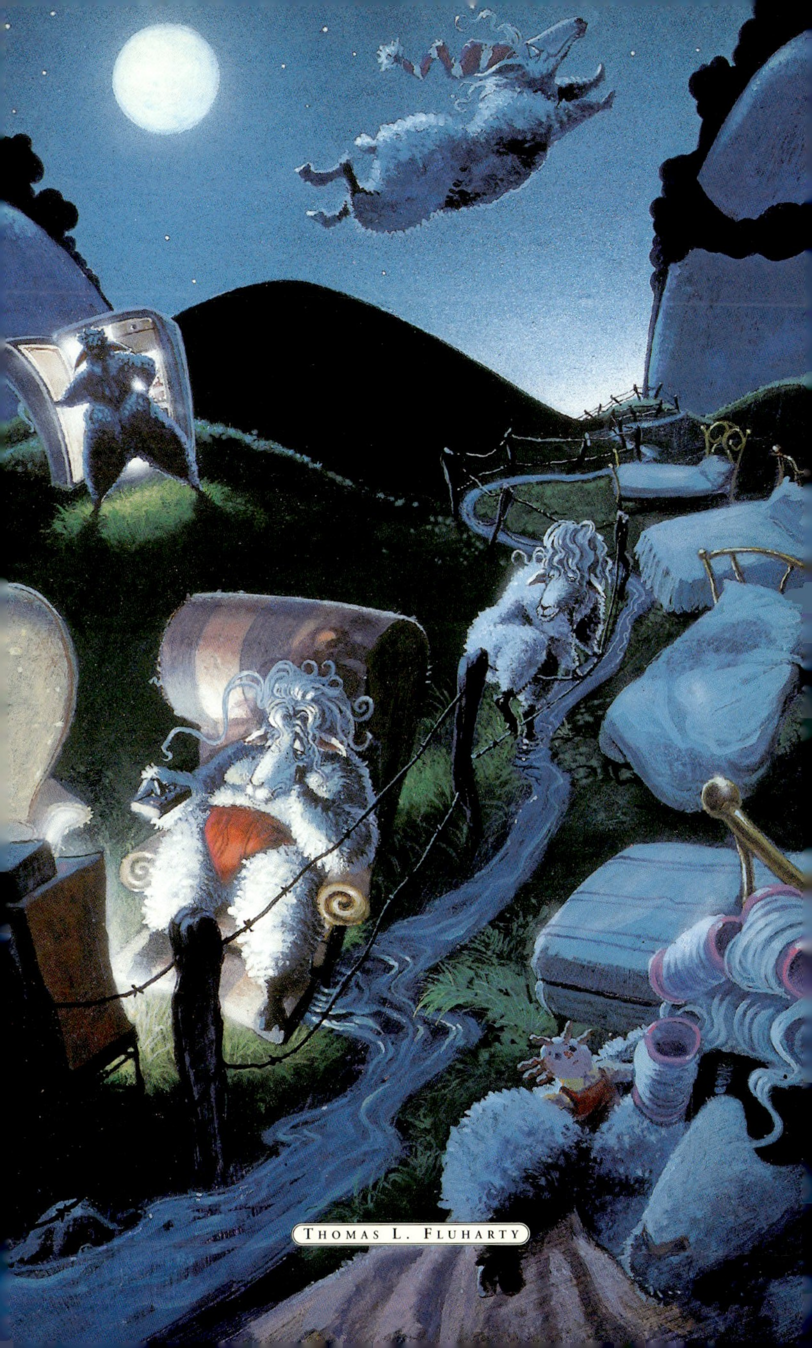
THOMAS L. FLUHARTY

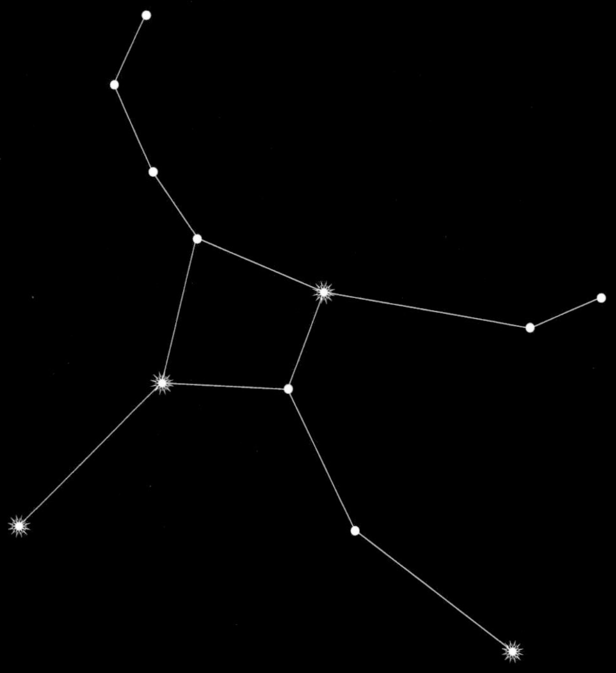

Hercules

93

NINETY-THREE

DREIUNDNEUNZIG

QUATRE-VINGT-TREIZE

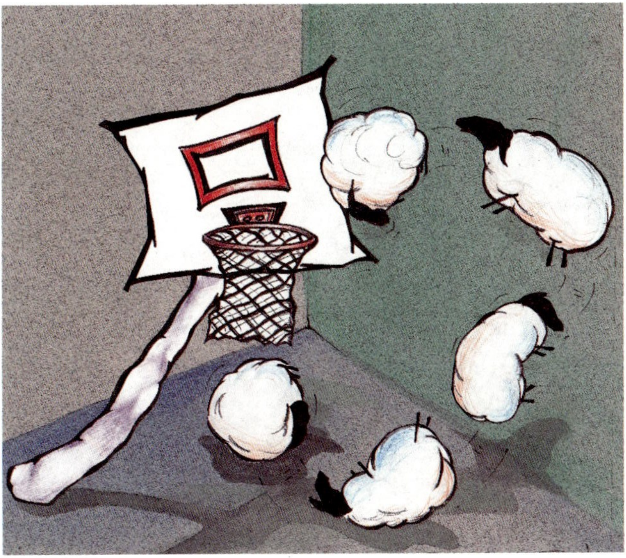

SHOMARI SMITH

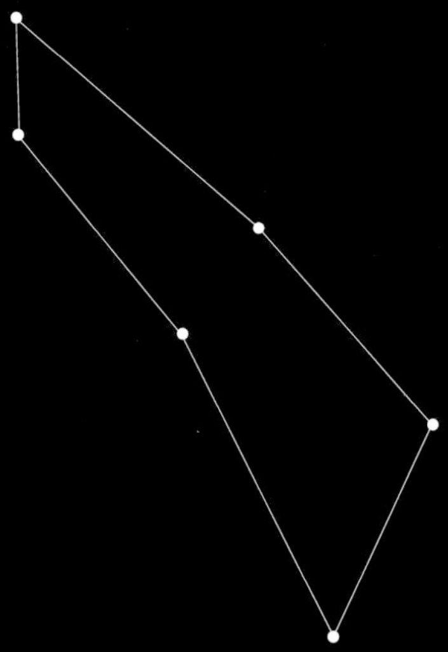

Lepus the Hare

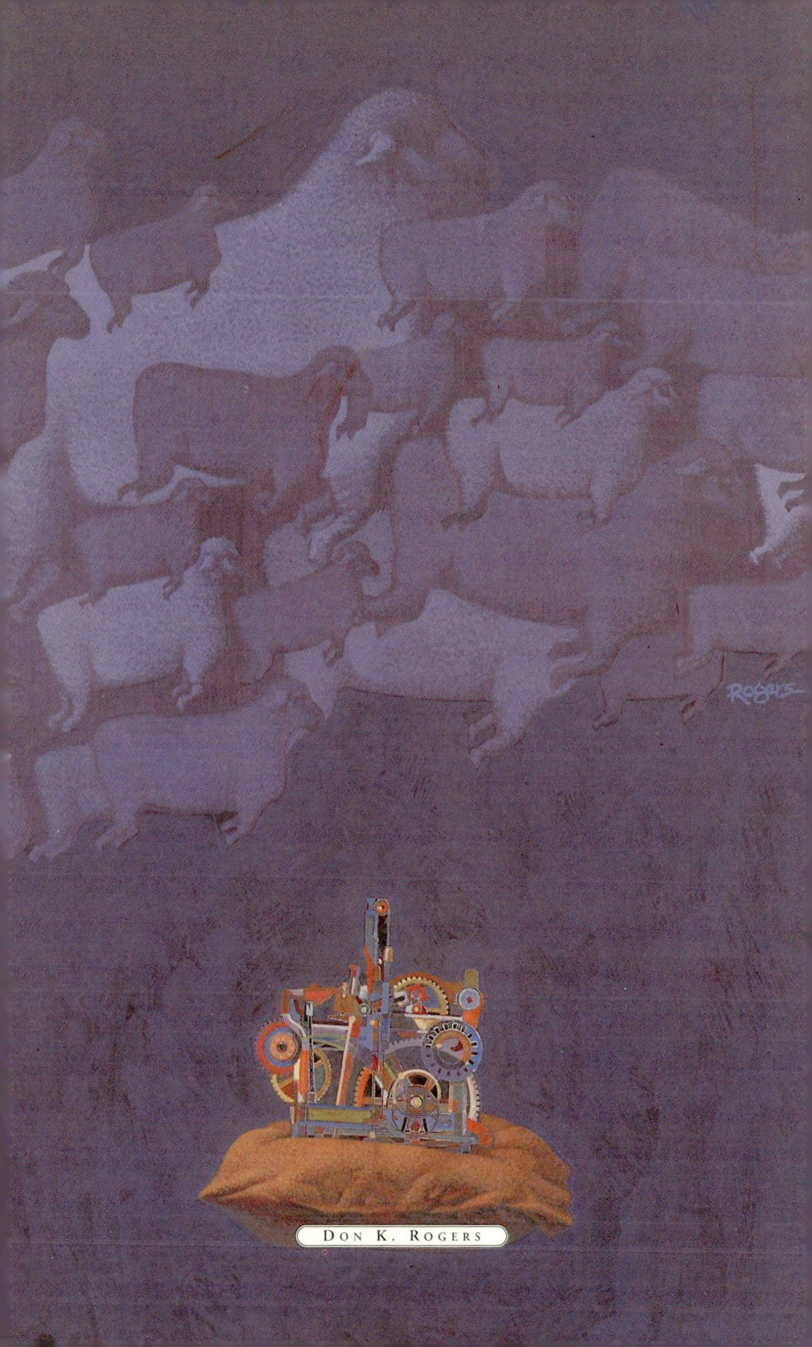
Rogers
DON K. ROGERS

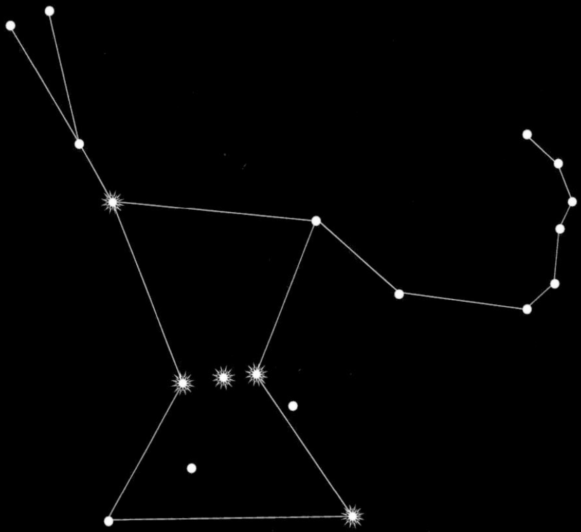

Orion the Hunter

97

NINETY-SEVEN

SIEBENUNDNEUNZIG

QUATRE-VINGT-DIX-SEPT

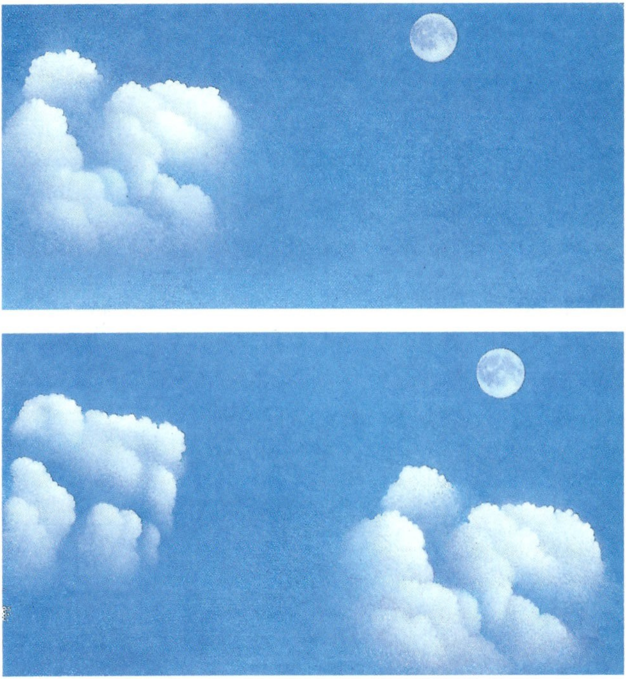

JACK ENDEWELT

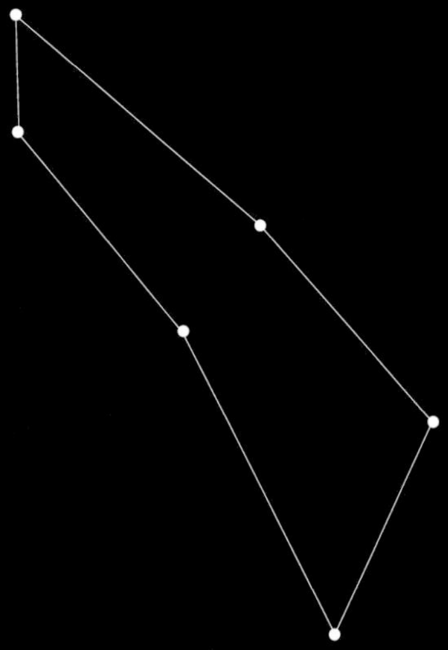

Lepus the Hare

99

NINETY-NINE

NEUNUNDNEUNZIG

QUATRE-VINGT-DIX-NEUF

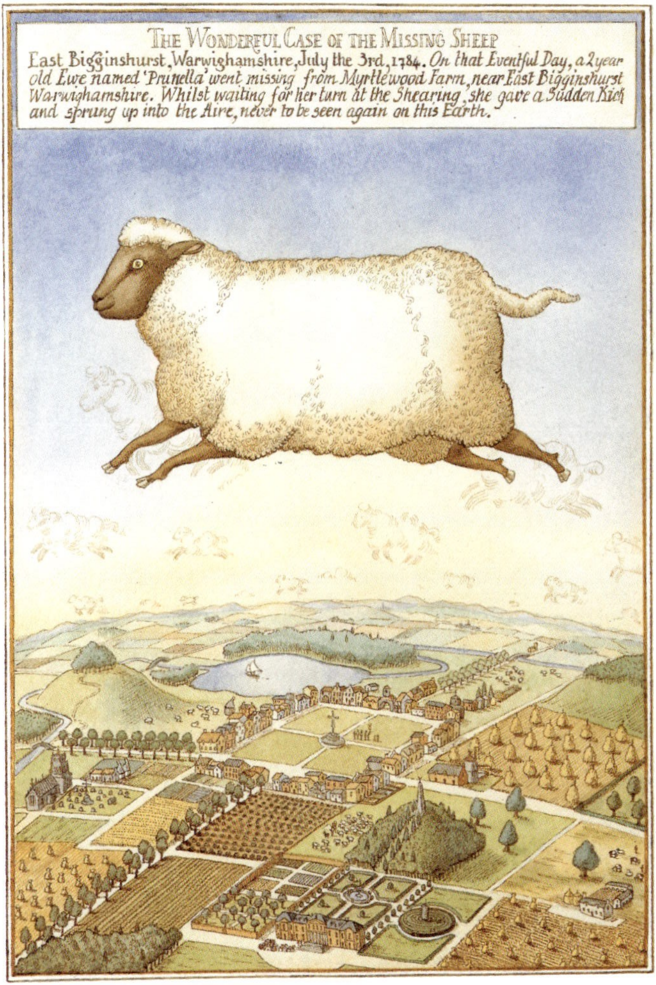

LAURA FILIPPUCCI

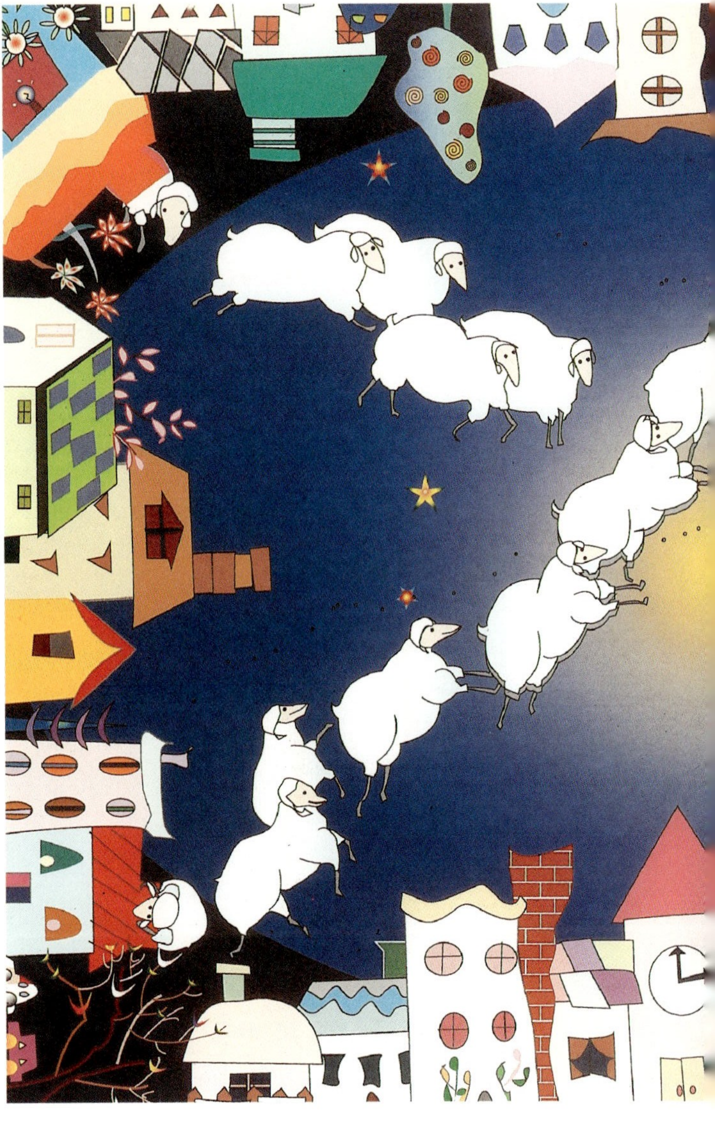

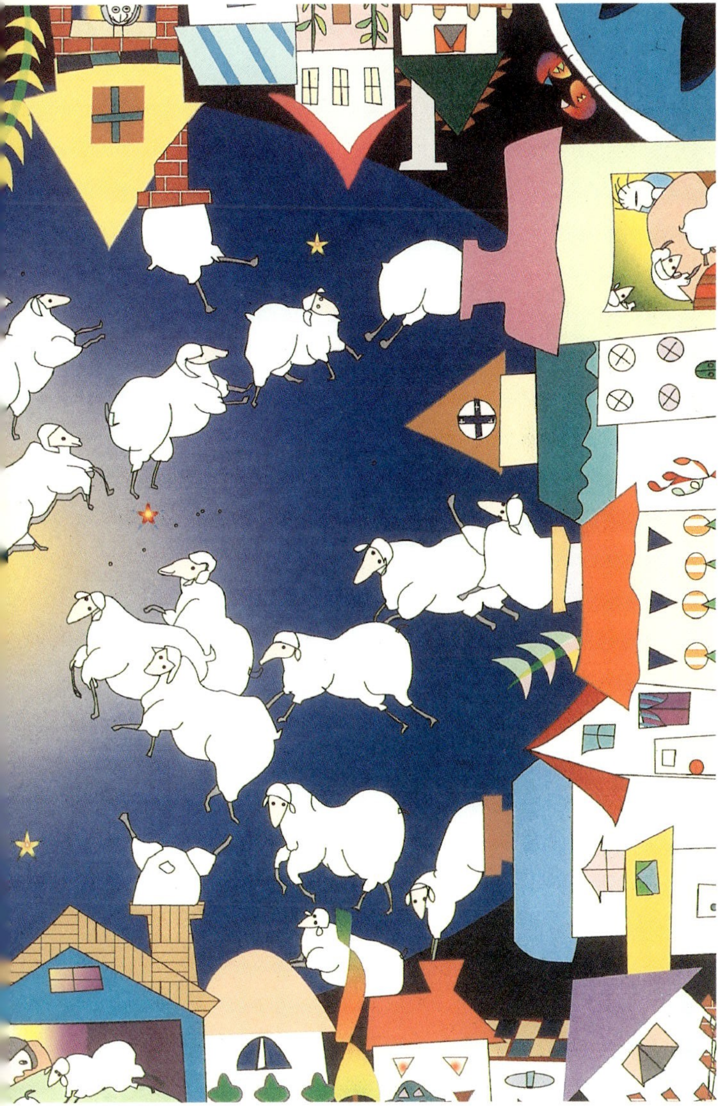

Yoonseon Choi

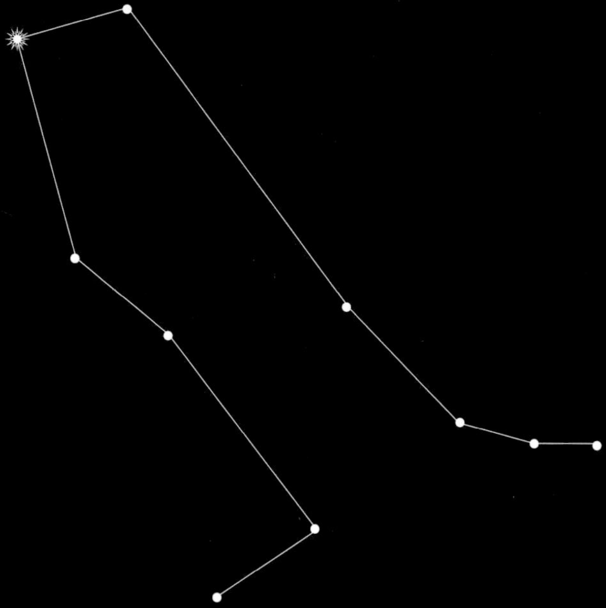

Gemini the Twins

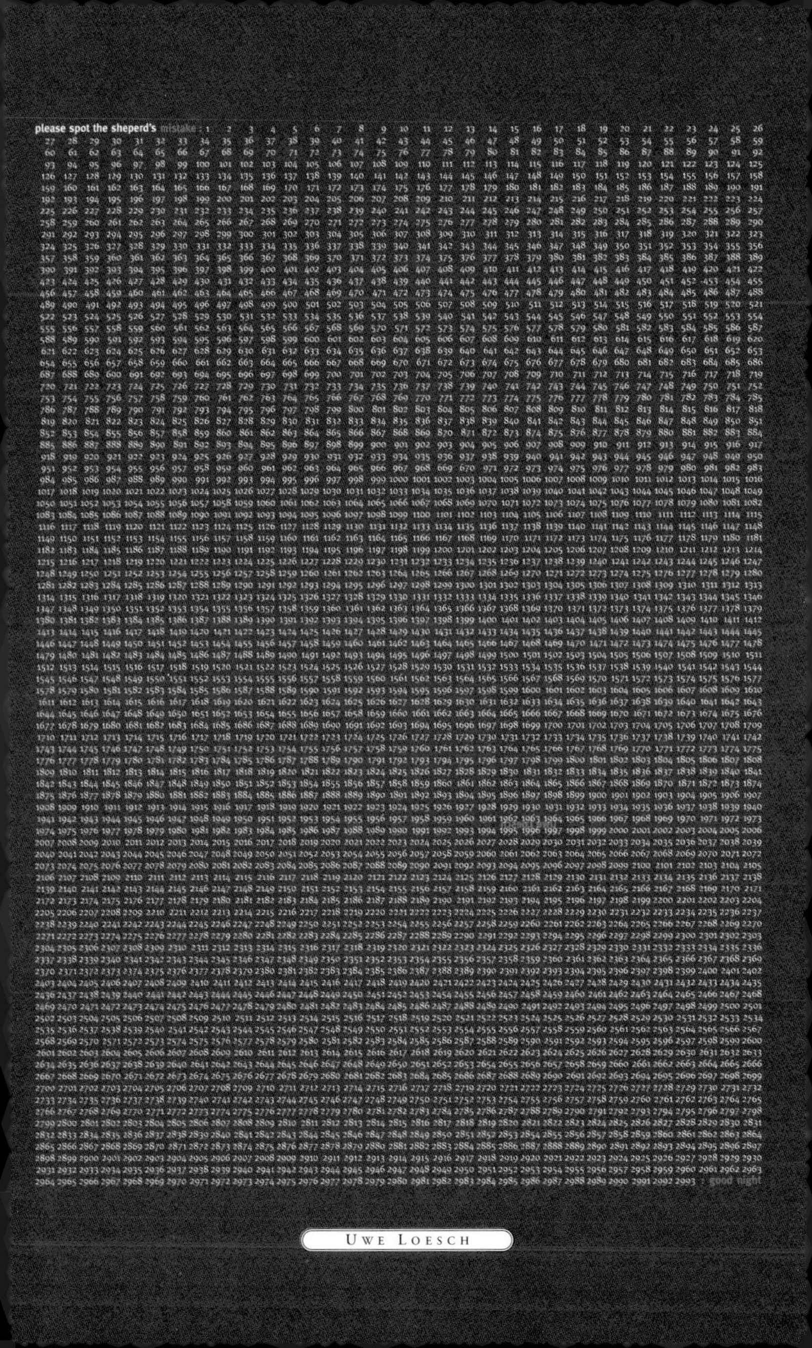
please spot the sheperd's mistake : 1 2 3 4 5 6 7 8 9 10 11 12 13 14 15 16 17 18 19 20 21 22 23 24 25 26
2984 2985 2986 2987 2988 2989 2990 2991 2992 2993 : good night
Uwe Loesch

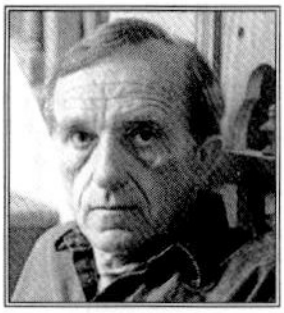

ED ABRAMS (P.83) LIVES IN JULIAN, CALIFORNIA. BORN IN CLEVELAND, OHIO, ABRAMS' FIRST JOB WAS WITH AMERICAN GREETINGS. HE LATER MOVED TO CALIFORNIA TO WORK IN ADVERTISING, AND IN 1978 HE STARTED DOING FREELANCE ILLUSTRATION WORK. HE IS KNOWN FOR PORTRAITS IN MAGAZINES AND ON ANGELS RECORDS. HIS "THREE SHEEP" ILLUSTRATION WAS DONE WITH A NEW TOY, THE ETCHING PRESS.

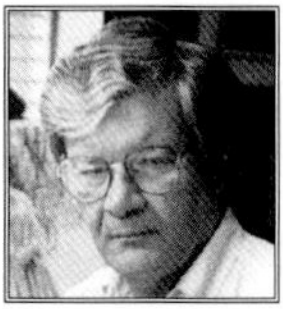

JAMES BARKLEY (P.71) WORKS AS AN ILLUSTRATOR AND FINE ART PAINTER FOR MAJOR CORPORATIONS, BOOK PUBLISHERS, AND ADVERTISING AGENCIES THROUGHOUT THE WORLD. AMONG HIS HONORS FOR NUMEROUS WORKS ARE AWARDS OF EXCELLENCE AND GOLD MEDALS FROM THE SOCIETY OF ILLUSTRATORS AND ART DIRECTORS CLUB. HE HAS ALSO HAD MANY ONE-MAN SHOWS THROUGHOUT THE NATION.

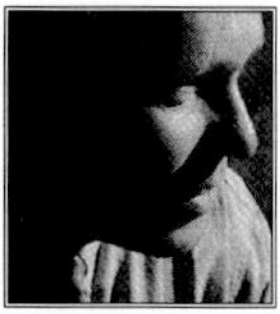

ROBERT BARRETT (P.63) IS A PAINTER, MURALIST, ILLUSTRATOR, AND PROFESSOR OF ILLUSTRATION AND CHAIR OF THE DESIGN DEPARTMENT AT BRIGHAM YOUNG UNIVERSITY. HE HAS EXHIBITED HIS WORK IN SEVERAL ART SHOWS, AND HIS CLIENTELE INCLUDES VIKING USA, RANDOM HOUSE, HARPER COLLINS, AND *MCCALLS*.

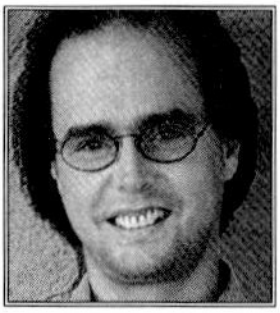

BRALDT BRALDS (P.21) IS AN ILLUSTRATOR WHO WORKED AS A TYPOGRAPHER IN HIS NATIVE HOLLAND IN THE 1960S. HE STARTED HIS DRAWING CAREER DOING ADVERTISING WORK FOR NEWSPAPERS. FOLLOWING A COVER ASSIGNMENT FOR *TIME* MAGAZINE, HE MOVED TO NEW YORK IN 1980. HIS WORK HAS RECEIVED NUMEROUS AWARDS AND HAS BEEN FEATURED IN MAJOR PUBLICATIONS, IN 1995 HE WAS INVITED TO SERVE ON THE INTERNATIONAL ADVISORY BOARD OF THE ART INSTITUTES INTERNATIONAL.

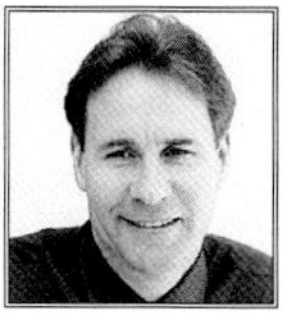

EDWARD J. BURKE (P.33) EARNED AN UNDERGRADUATE DEGREE IN SCULPTURE/CERAMICS FROM THE UNIVERSITY OF GEORGIA, AND A MASTER IN FINE ARTS FROM THE STATE UNIVERSITY OF NEW PALTZ, NEW YORK. HE HAS EXHIBITED IN ONE- AND TWO-PERSON SHOWS INTERNATIONALLY, AND SINCE 1978 HAS BEEN REPRESENTED BY THE WORK GALLERY IN NEW YORK. SINCE 1975 HE HAS BEEN PROFESSOR OF ART AT SUFFOLK COMMUNITY COLLEGE, SELDEN, NEW YORK. HE LIVES IN QUOGUE, LONG ISLAND, NEW YORK.

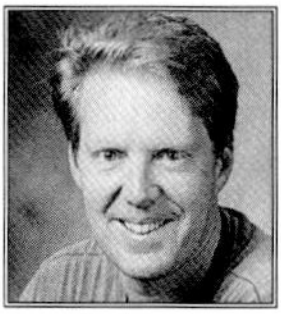

PATRICK CAMPBELL (P.49) EARNED A BACHELOR OF FINE ARTS IN ILLUSTRATION FROM BRIGHAM YOUNG UNIVERSITY. HE IS CURRENTLY ILLUSTRATING A CHILDREN'S BOOK FOR WATERFORD INSTITUTE, AS WELL AS DOING FREELANCE EDITORIAL WORK. CAMPBELL, HIS WIFE, AND THEIR FIVE CHILDREN RESIDE IN OREM, UTAH.

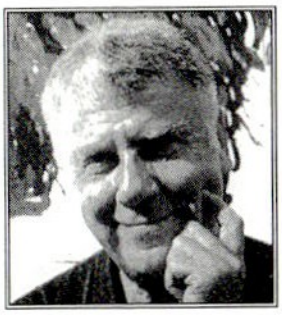

BILL CHARMATZ (P.67)
Born in New York City, Charmatz studied and started his career in Paris. He has done illustration since 1945 for clients such as *Harper's Bazaar, The New York Times*, IBM, *Sports Illustrated*, and American Express. He has written and illustrated several children's books, TV commercials, and other projects, and has won numerous awards.

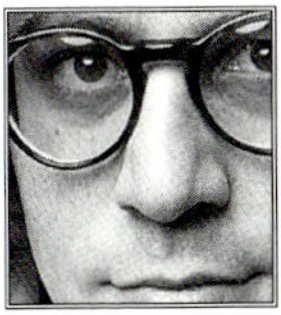

© DAN NELKEN

DAVID CHELSEA (P.19)
After spending half his life in New York, Chelsea recently returned to Portland, Oregon, and divides his time between free-lance illustration—for clients including *Spy, Newsweek*, and *Readers Digest*—and his comic work. He has written and illustrated two graphic novels and is working on an instructional book for cartoonists and illustrators.

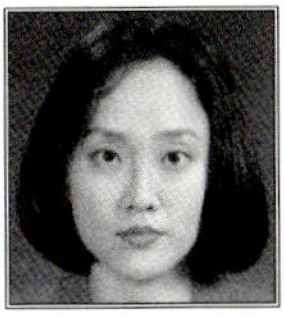

YOONSEON CHOI
(P.100/101) is a junior at California College of Arts and Crafts in Oakland, pursuing a Bachelor of Arts in illustration. She has earned a Bachelor of Arts in Philosophy from Ehwa Woman's University in Seoul, Korea. She resides with her husband, David Lee, in Redwood City, California.

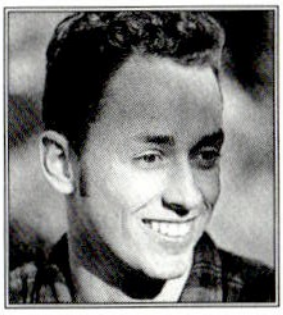

CRAIG COOK (P.15)
Since his graduation from Somerset College of Art in 1989, Cook has worked in London on C.I. and literature projects. His design work for annual reports has won design and communication awards on both sides of the Atlantic. While working at Identica Cook has developed large literature systems for several clients. Meanwhile he has continued to maintain his pastime of alpine climbing and mountaineering.

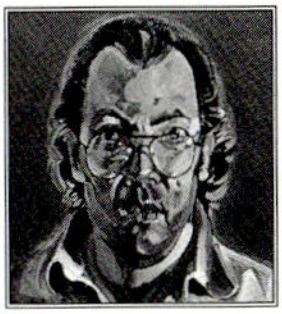

ABE ECHEVARRIA
(P.27) studied at the School of Art and Design, the Academy of Fine Arts, and the School of Visual Arts. He is an experienced art director and Illustrator whose work has been shown in several exhibitions, including the Society of Illustrators 18th Annual, 27th Annual (where he was a Gold Medal Winner), and the New York Historical Society. He is currently Associate Professor and Chairman of the Art Department at Western Connecticut State University, and he resides in New Milford,Connecticut.

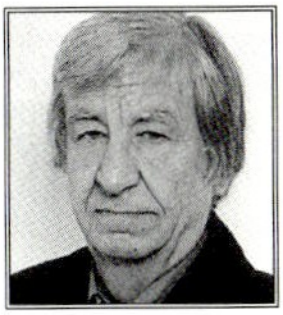

HEINZ EDELMANN
(P.43) has been a free-lance graphic designer since 1959. He has also worked in the fields of illustration and animation, and he has taught at several art schools; he currently teaches in Stuttgart.

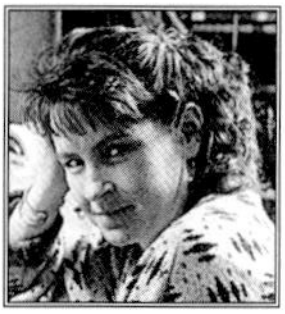

KATHI EMBER (P.9,45) lives in an old stone farmhouse in Pennsylvania with one man, two horses, three sheep and four cats. For over 15 years, her illustrations have appeared in books and magazines. She claims that sheep make great pets and lawn mowers, despite the fact that they are somewhat mentally challenged.

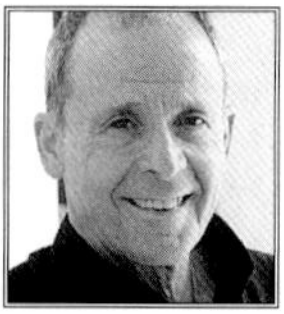

JACK ENDEWELT (P.97) has been a working illustrator since 1961, in books, magazines, paperback covers, children's books and advertising in the United States, Great Britain, South America and Japan. In 1987 he participated in his first group exhibit in a gallery and has been painting and exhibiting ever since. He received a silver medal in the 1995 Society of Illustrators Show. He is Chair of Illustration and Cartooning at the School of Visual Arts.

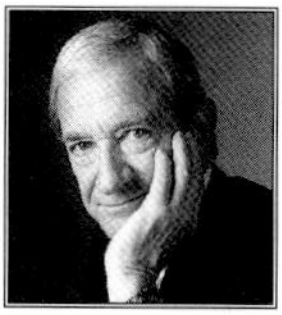

GENE FEDERICO (P.31) in 1991 opened his consultancy practice, in contemporary marketing via advertising and graphic design, areas in which he has contributed many years of award-winning work for a wide variety of agencies and clients. He has been honored as an Art Directors Hall of Fame Laureate, an AIGA Medalist, an Honorary Doctorate recipient from the New School at Parsons, an Achievement Award winner from Pratt Institute and a Type Directors Club Medalist.

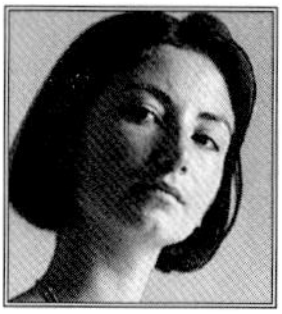

LAURA FILIPPUCCI (P.99) was born in Milano, Italy, where she completed Classical Studies, then graduated from the European Institute of Design in 1985. Since then, she's been freelancing in Italy, the UK, and the USA as a children's book and magazine illustrator.

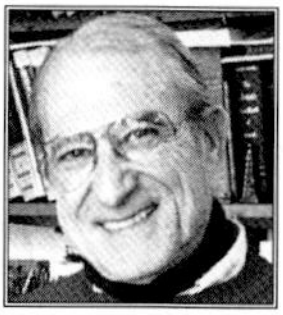

LEONARD EVERETT FISHER (P.37) was born in New York City in 1924 and began his art training eight years later at the Heckscher Foundation. He attended Yale University's School of Art, and served as assistant instructor in design at Yale. After receiving the Pulitzer painting award in 1950, he began a diversified career as a painter, author, illustrator, designer and educator. He is Dean Emeritus of Paier College of Art in Connecticut.

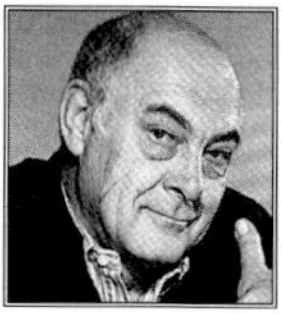

ALAN FLETCHER (P.55) is one of the founding partners of the international design firm Pentagram, and now an independent designer whose reputation is reflected by commissions from major corporations and cultural institutions around the world. He is also an artist with a wide-ranging portfolio of illustrations.

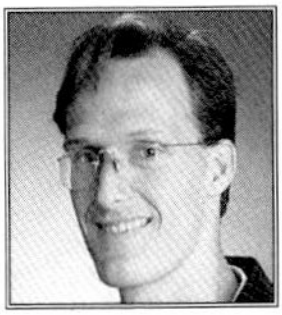

THOMAS L. FLUHARTY (P.91) studied illustration at the Art Institute of Pittsburgh. He has spent the past 12 years in New York City working for major advertising agencies. He was recently commissioned to do his first cover for *Mad* magazine. Fluharty and his wife live with their three children in Manhattan.

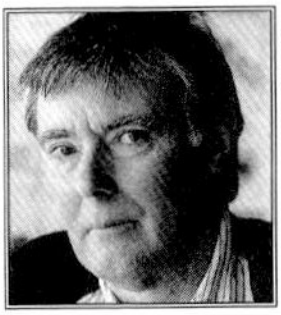

© MALCOLM CROWTHERS

DAVID GENTLEMAN (P.85) is an artist and designer whose work includes painting in watercolor, lithography, and wood engraving. He has designed stamps, posters and a mural on the London subway, and has written and published five books of his own watercolors, about Britain, London, the British coastline, Paris, and India. He is currently working on a book about Italy. Gentleman lives in London.

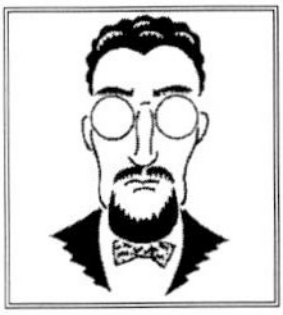

STEVEN GUARNACCIA (P.23) is an illustrator and designer whose work has appeared in books and magazines, greeting cards, clothing, rugs, and jewelry. His drawings appear in *The New York Times* and other publications. He has illustrated two collections of palindromes, *Madam I'm Adam* and *If I had a Hifi*. He has had several one-person shows and received numerous awards. He teaches a class, "The Satiric Image," at the School of Visual Arts.

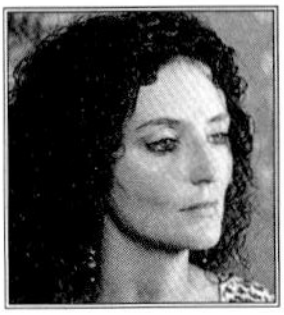

TRACI HAYMANS (P.87) is an illustrator and educator living and working in the Deep South. Her work has been featured in *Yankee* magazine, *Recorded Books*, *Outside* magazine and various other publications. Haymans teaches illustration at the Savannah College of Art and Design in Georgia.

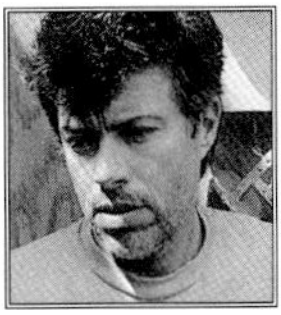

© JASON PENDREY

TERRY HOFF (P.41) was the winner of the 1994 California Discovery Award Gold Medal, and the Grand Prize at the San Diego Art Institute's 40th International competition. His work is included in many corporate and private collections. He creates fine art and advertising images from his studio in Pacifica, California.

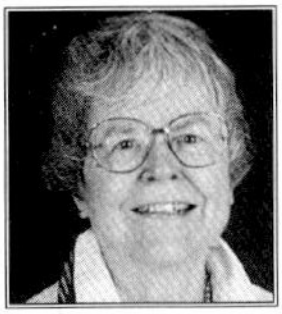

GINNIE HOFMANN (P.47) was born in Toledo, Ohio, and studied at the Art Academy of Cincinnati. She has been an illustrator in New York for 25 years, with clients including the *McCall's* children's page, *Mademoiselle*, and numerous advertising agencies. She is the Author and illustrator of four children's books for Random House, with a fifth book currently in progress. She is a member of the Society of Illustrators.

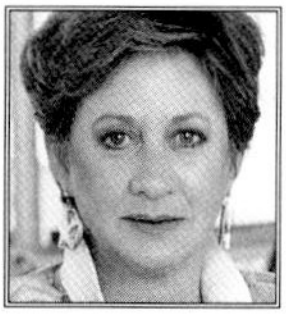

JOYCE KITCHELL (P.57) is a watercolor artist residing in San Diego. She has created editorial illustrations, posters, gift items, calendars, dinnerware, illustrations for national corporations, book covers, a children's book and cookbooks. Her work has won packaging awards for many products and has appeared in several publications and the Society of Illustrators New York and Los Angeles exhibitions.

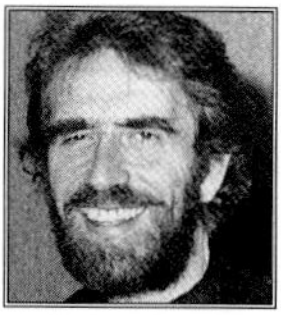

UWE LOESCH (P.103) was born in Germany, and has a studio in Dusseldorf, He is professor for Communication Design at the University in Wuppertal. He has won many prizes at international poster biennials, including the Grand Prix in Lahti, Finland. His work has been in one man exhibitions and publications worldwide, and since 1983 he is represented in the Museum of Modern Art in New York City.

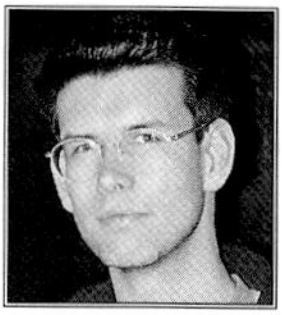

SIMON MANCHIPP (P.53) is a London-based designer. He graduated with a 1st class degree in Graphic Design from St. Martins School of Art. His typography has been featured in numerous exhibitions and magazines, and he has worked for the design group Identica and currently HHCL&P, dealing with multimedia, print, type design, packaging, and television.

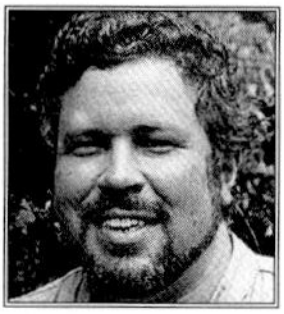

KEVIN KRENECK (P.59) After 10 years as a newspaper staff artist, Kevin Kreneck became a freelance illustrator in 1992. He has received recognition from The Society of Newspaper Design and The Society of Illustrators, and his work appears in exhibitions and surveys. He is syndicated by the Los Angeles Times Op-Art Syndicate.

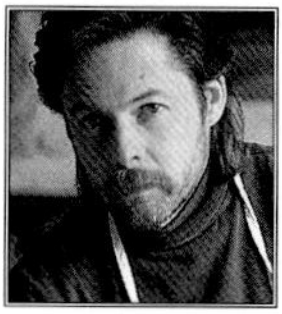

GREGORY MANCHESS (P.77) recently returned from an expedition with *National Geographic*, and often travels to study subjects for clients and gallery work. An admirer of 19th century painters, his work has graced book covers, magazines, and cinematic projects. A native Kentuckian, he makes the Pacific Northwest his home.

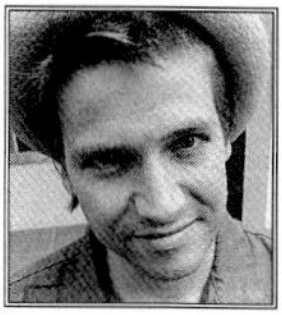

© CYNTHIA WIGGINTON

ADAM MCCAULEY (P.75) is an Oakland, California-based illustrator and musician. Born in Berkeley, California, and raised in Missouri, McCauley received a Bachelor of Fine Arts in Illustration from Parsons in New York City. After long days of drawing for various huge and tiny magazines, newspapers, record covers, books, and an occasional clock, he drums in his weird band, Little My.

BIOGRAPHIES

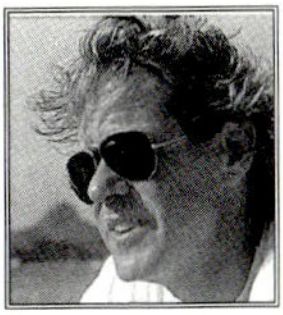

JON McINTOSH (P.2) has been a freelance illstrator and designer in the Boston area for 25 years. Awards include a Silver Funny Bone from the Society of Illustrators and Gold Medals from the Society of Newspaper Designers.

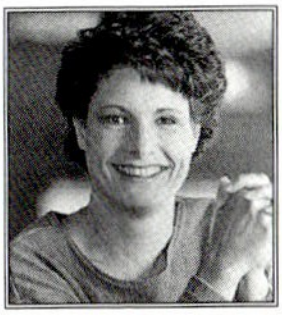

DIANA MCKNIGHT (P.11) and her husband, Joseph Rattan, are principal designers and partners at Joseph Rattan Design in Dallas, Texas. She is a graduate of Texas Tech University. McKnight has been recognized in numerous design shows and publications.

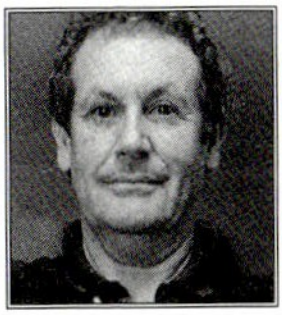

JONATHAN MILNE (P.13) draws dimensional illustrations which have been included in print and television spots, reproduced in Canada, USA, Germany, England, Scotland, Italy, Ireland, Singapore and Australia. A member of the Society of Illustrators, New York, and the Association of Illustrators, London, he is also a feature artist in a Ziegler/Greco book on paper sculpture. Born in Melbourne, Australia, he has worked and lived in Canada for 20 years.

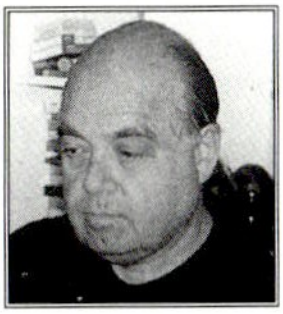

GEOFFREY MOSS (P.29) is a conceptual illustrator whose satirical newspaper drawings are internationally syndicated by *The Washington Post*. Other credits include designing theater sets and posters, writing, lecturing, teaching and illustrating children's books. With his schedule he would like nothing better than to count sheep.

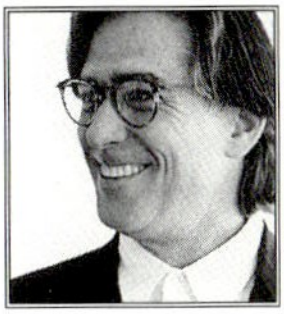

© PETER HARRISON

WOODY PIRTLE (P.7) studied Architecture and Fine Art. He is a graphic design consultant who joined Pentagram in 1988 as a partner, following ten years of running his own practice in Dallas and previous training with The Richards Group. His work is included in the permanent collections of the Museum of Modern Art, the Cooper-Hewitt National Museum of Design, and the Zurich Poster Museum.

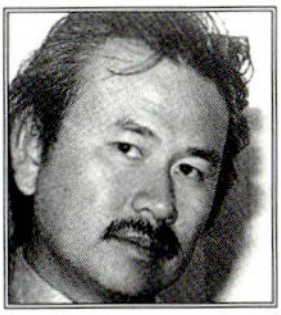

MIKE QUON (P.79) is a native of Los Angeles whose New York City design office has earned an international reputation for distinctive solutions. His work has been exhibited throughout the world.

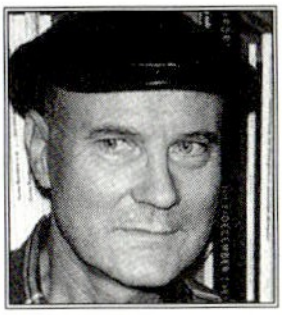

GUNTER RAMBOW (P.25) Since the 1960s, Professor Rambow has been a distinguished international poster designer. His posters are represented in many important poster collections and are widely exhibited.

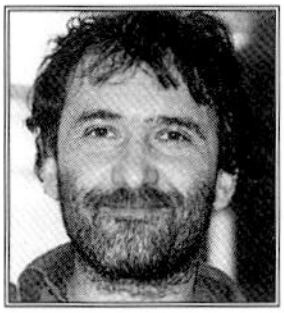

ROBERT RAYEVSKY (P.65) was born in Moscow in the time of the Cold War. In 1979 he moved to New York City. An award-winning illustrator of 17 children's books, he recently added to his interests the creation of editorial and advertising illustrations. He is represented by Salzman International. Rayevsky and his family currently live in North Wales, Pennsylvania.

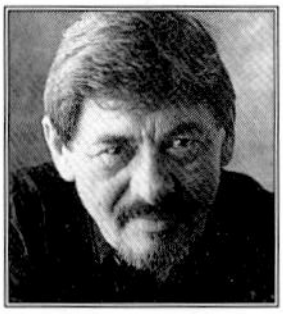

DAN REISINGER (P.61) is a graphic communicatory who lives in Israel, which he has called home since 1949. He studied at Bezalel Academy in Jerusalem, and at Central School of Art in London. He has worked in cities including Brussels, London, and New York, and he is a member of Alliance Graphique International and the Art Directors Club, New York.

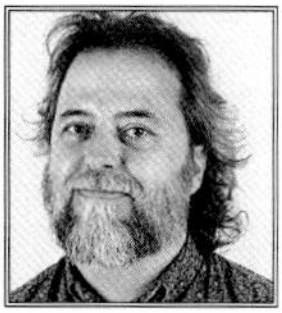

DON K. ROGERS (P.95) is currently living in Savannah, Georgia, where he is Chair of the Illustration Department at the Savannah College Art and Design. Since 1978, he has been an illustrator working with clients ranging from Turner Broadcasting to GTE, and he continues a combination of teaching and freelance work.

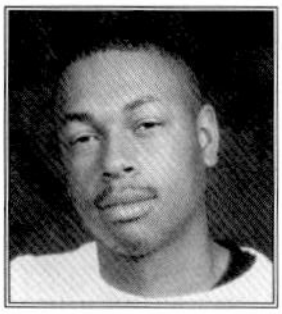

SHOMARI SMITH (P.93) was born in Oakland, California, and is an illustration student at California College of Arts and Crafts, He has served as a television director and production assistant for projects including the Oakland Unified School District, KTOP City of Oakland, and the Oakland Museum Video youth focus on Oakland Community Animation Project. His honors include the Tom Hanks Golden Apple Award in 1995.

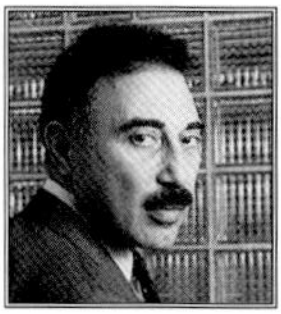

HENRY STEINER (P.89) was born in Vienna, raised in New York, and educated at Hunter College, Yale University, and the Sorbonne. In 1964 he founded Graphic Communication Ltd.—later Steiner & Co.—in Hong Kong. He is president of Alliance Graphique Internationale, a fellow of the Chartered Society of Designers and the New York Art Directors Club. He has recently co-authored a new book, *Cross-Cultural Design*, published in 1995.

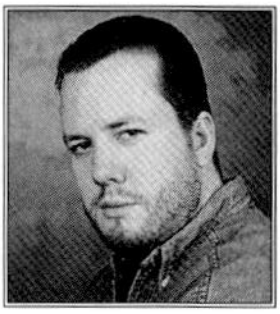

RANDY STUART (P.17) is a freelance illustrator based in Provo, Utah. He has a bachelor of arts degree in design from Brigham Young University with an emphasis in illustration. He has worked extensively in computer graphics for educational software, but painting remains his first love.

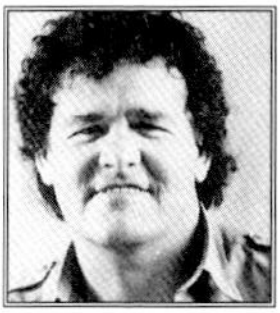

PAUL SZEP (P.73) IS EDITORIAL CARTOONIST FOR *THE BOSTON GLOBE*. HIS AWARDS INCLUDE THE PULITZER PRIZE (TWICE), THE INTERNATIONAL THOMAS NAST AWARD, AND THREE HONORARY DOCTORATES. HE HAS PUBLISHED 12 BOOKS, AND IS ALSO A FELLOW AT HARVARD UNIVERSITY. HE IS A REGULAR CONTRIBUTOR TO *GOLF DIGEST*. HE LIVES IN BROOKLINE, MASSACHUSSETTS, AND HAS TWO CHILDREN, AMY AND JASON.

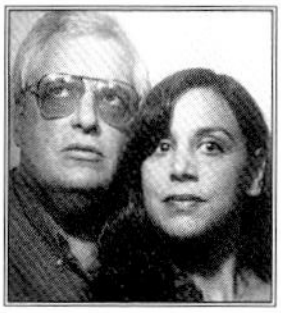

TWO MAN SAW (P.35) IS A DUO OF ILLUSTRATORS AND DESIGNERS—COMPOSED OF LARS HOKANSON AND FRANCES CICHETTI—BASED IN PHILADELPHIA. THEIR PRIMARY TECHNIQUE IS WOODCUT, AND THEIR INFLUENCES INCLUDE ITALIAN AND JAPANESE DESIGN AND ARTWORK. TWO MAN SAW'S WORK INCLUDES ADVERTISING, PUBLISHING AND EDITORIAL PROJECTS, AS WELL AS PROFESSORSHIP AT THE UNIVERSITY OF THE ARTS.

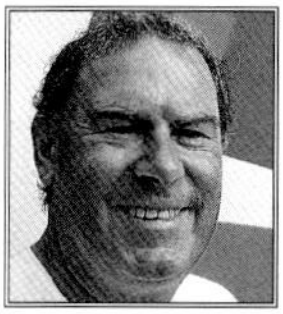

NIKLAUS TROXLER (P.69) IS WORKING AS GRAPHIC DESIGNER AND ARTIST IN WILLISAU, SWITZERLAND. HE IS THE RECIPIENT OF MANY AWARDS AND PRIZES FOR HIS POSTERS AND IS ALSO KNOWN FOR HIS GRAFFITIS AS WELL AS HIS TEXTILE AND WATCH DESIGNS. HE IS THE ORGANIZOR OF THE INTERNATIONAL JAZZ FESTIVAL IN WILLISAU.

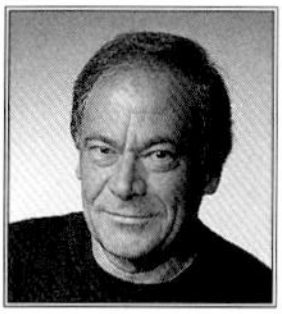

© STEVE KEOUGH

BARRIE TUCKER (P.51) IS AN AUSTRALIAN DESIGNER RENOWNED FOR HIS WINE PACKAGING DESIGN. HIS AWARDS INCLUDE GOLD AND SILVER CLIOS 1995 FOR WINE PACKAGING, THE WORLD STAR PACK AWARD 1995, AND FIRST PRIZE (OF THE CULTURAL SECTION) AT THE POSTER BIENNALE IN LAHTI, FINLAND. HIS WORK WAS ALSO FEATURED ON THE COVER OF *GRAPHIS* MAGAZINE (190) AND IN A ONE-MAN RETROSPECTIVE EXHIBITION AT THE AXIS DESIGN CENTER IN TOKYO IN 1991.

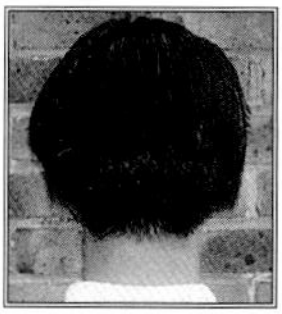

JIMMY YANG (P.39) WAS BORN IN HONG KONG AND GRADUATED FROM CANTERBURY COLLEGE OF ART. HE JOINED THE LONDON-BASED DESIGN CONSULTANCY LEWIS MOBERLY IN 1986 BEFORE HIS APPOINTMENT AS CREATIVE DIRECTOR OF IDENTICA IN 1992. HIS WORK HAS WON NUMEROUS INTERNATIONAL AWARDS AND HAS BEEN FEATURED IN SEVERAL PROFESSIONAL DESIGN ANNUALS.

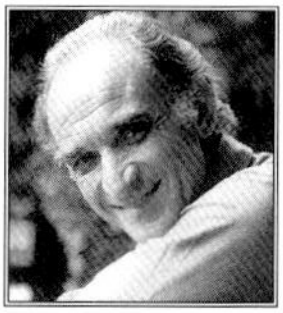

BOB ZIERING (P.81) HAS BEEN COMMISSIONED BY PROMINENT CORPORATIONS, AGENCIES, PUBLISHERS AND INDIVIDUALS FOR MORE THAN 30 YEARS. HIS ILLUSTRATION WORK HAS BEEN FEATURED IN SEVERAL ONE-MAN EXHIBITIONS, WITH PRESENTORS AND SPONSORS INCLUDING THE NEW YORK SOCIETY OF ILLUSTRATORS, THE UNITED NATIONS, AND THE NEW YORK ZOOLOGICAL SOCIETY IN AN EVENT AT THE CENTRAL PARK ZOO.

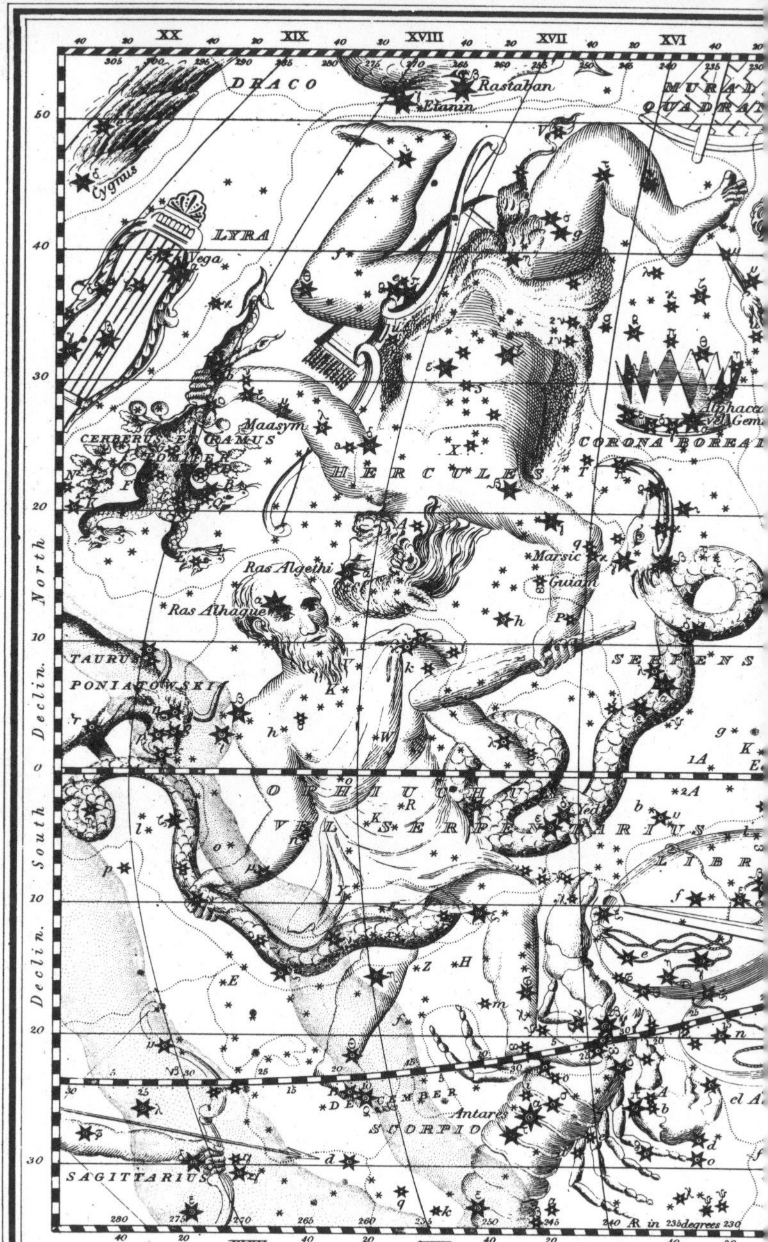

XX
XIX
XVIII
XVII
XVI
DRACO
Rastaban
Etanin
MURAL QUADRANT
Cygnus
LYRA
Vega
HERCULES
Maasym
CERBERUS ET RAMUS POMIFER
CORONA BOREALIS
Alphacca
Ras Algethi
Ras Alhague
Marsic
Guiam
TAURUS PONIATOWSKI
SERPENS
OPHIUCHUS VEL SERPENTARIUS
LIBRA
DECEMBER
Antares
SCORPIO
SAGITTARIUS
North Declin.
South Declin.
Æ in degrees
Æ in time